LETTING PEOPLE OFF THE HOOK

Jessie Rice Sandberg

VICTOR BOOKS

A DIVISION OF SCRIPTURE PRESS PUBLICATIONS INC.
USA CANADA ENGLAND

"Trust His Heart," by Eddie Carswell and Babbie Mason is used by permission. © Copyright 1989 by May Sun Music (adm. by Word Music), Causing Change Music (adm. by Dayspring Music), Word Music & Dayspring Music (both DIVS. OF WORD, INC.). All Rights Reserved.

Quotation reprinted from *Walking on Water* by Madeleine L'Engle is used by permission of Harold Shaw Publishers, Wheaton, IL. © 1980 by Crosswick.

Scripture quotations are from the *Holy Bible, New International Version®*. Copyright © 1973, 1978, 1984 by International Bible Society. Used by permission of Zondervan Publishing House. All rights reserved. Other quotations are from the *Authorized (King James) Version* (KJV).

Copyediting: Carole Streeter and Barbara Williams
Cover Design: Andrea Boven

Library of Congress Cataloging-in-Publication Data

Sandberg, Jessie Rice.
    Letting people off the hook / by Jessie R. Sandberg.
      p.   cm.
    ISBN: 1-56476-418-4 (pbk.)
    1. Forgiveness–Religious aspects–Christianity. 2. Forgiveness of sin.
3. Christian life. I. Title.
BV4647.F55S26 1995
234'.5–dc20   95-2482
                                                 CIP

---

1 2 3 4 5 6 7 8 9 10 Printing/Year 99 98 97 96 95

To my favorite people

Sandy
Carol and Roger
Jim and Jennifer
Don and Kay
Mark

PURPOSE OF BOOK

n my years of counseling and teaching, and rearing my own four children, I have come to the realization that nearly all of us carry around unfinished business—a lack of forgiveness. Some have faced major heartache in their lives, and it is easy for them to view their unforgiveness as "justified." Others carry around "grudge books" in their minds and these get heavier day by day as they collect the daily grievances of living in a damaged world.

Most unforgiveness, I find, is unacknowledged and therefore is allowed to fester in the soul until every part of life has been contaminated by its poison.

"I consider myself to be a happy, loving person," a waitress said to me the other day, "and if somebody hurts me I can dismiss it pretty quickly the first time. But if they ever do the same thing a second time, then that's it! I never let a person hurt me twice!"

Her viewpoint, I think, is a typical one. Most of us believe in forgiveness at some primary level, but we do not know how to practice it as a way of life.

This book is for all of us—those who have been deeply hurt by some sin which they see as "unforgivable" and those who simply have trouble letting people be what they are in the daily pressures of life.

CONTENTS

Introduction   9

1. A Lost Eden 11

2. Why Forgiveness Is So Hard 21

3. Why We Absolutely Must Forgive 29

4. When Confrontation Is in Order 39

5. Building Patterns of Forgiveness......................51

6. Being "Human" and Being "Evil"......................63

7. The Goal of Discipline and Forgiveness:
   Restoration 75

8. Is Any Sin Unforgivable? 85

9. Forgiveness and the Character of God.................99

10. Is Forgiveness Always Instant and
    Permanent? 109

11. Words! Words! Words! Why Forgiveness
    Must Be Verbal..121

12. Why Grieving Is Essential to Forgiving............. 131

13. The Home: God's Graduate Course in
    Forgiveness...147

14. How to Get Even: Design Your Own
    "Hit List" 161

15. Letting Yourself off the Hook 173

16. Letting God off the Hook............................... 185

17. Love: The Ultimate Revenge 197

    Notes   207

INTRODUCTION

This is a book about beginnings—not endings. It is about the *first* step all of us must make in the process of finding solutions to the problem of living in a sinful world. It certainly will not guarantee an end to the pain of heartache or disappointment because of "man's inhumanity to man." It will not eliminate the necessity of having to deal with—over and over again—the anger and hurt that come with living in a flawed world where human beings, even those who love each other, cause pain.

But perhaps a study of the options available will make it possible for us to build a lifestyle of responding in the best way possible to every encounter with malice or unfairness or thoughtlessness. That is the purpose of this book.

Obviously, letting people off the hook when they have hurt us is not a "natural" response. It involves an end result that is far from common—a response to evil intent or violence or indifference that is possible only through the grace and power of God. It involves a response that requires not a cringing spinelessness in the face of wrong, but the courage to handle wrong in a way that glorifies God and brings great peace of heart, even in the midst of suffering.

Although this is not a book about endings, I would not

want you to believe that God does not ultimately resolve what is wrong, or bring to a just conclusion the things that seem unfair. God's tender reassurances to the Israelites in their time of great distress are as true for His children today as they were for those early Jews. " 'For I know the plans I have for you,' declares the Lord, 'plans to prosper you and not to harm you, plans to give you hope and a future' " (Jeremiah 29:11).

Still, forgiveness is not a conditional quality we measure out to others only in terms of a guaranteed resolution to mistreatment or pain. In a sense we are responding with forgiveness on the basis of what it will do for us, the for-givers, rather than what it will do for the ones we forgive. That is the "ending" we must leave with God. What we *can* do, and what God *expects* us to do, is to learn how to forgive, repeatedly and genuinely, those who have caused us pain.

JESSIE RICE SANDBERG

ONE

A LOST EDEN

Sometimes, when my husband and I are taking our morning walk through Chickamauga National Park, I try to imagine what it would have been like to live in the Garden of Eden. On a beautiful, clear summer day, it is not hard to pretend I am there. The air is heavy with the fragrance of honeysuckle; wild daisies and Queen Anne's lace and buttercups line the sides of the road. Bright cardinals play a game of tag in the cedars; occasionally deer, some of them wearing yellow tags attached to their ears by the forest rangers, peek at us through the trees.

But when I look closely, there are obvious signs of a world damaged by sin's curse. Diseased trees lie fallen; a dead crow on the trail draws flies. Beautiful as the animals are that inhabit the forest, there is no pleasant interchange between breed and breed, nor is there fellowship between the animals and the hundreds of human beings who walk or bike or drive through the forest every day. Always there is an awareness of predator and prey. There is fear.

Other signs make it clear that this is no Eden. In nearly every little glade and beside every road are monuments and markers indicating that the bloodiest battle of the Civil War was fought here, with the loss of more than

30,000 Union and Confederate soldiers in one day. Historians say that the creek ran red with the blood of those who died. What carnage in my Eden!

In all literature, sacred and secular, we can trace man's search for another Eden. Some have called it The Lost Atlantis, Shangri-La, Brigadoon, Camelot or simply "somewhere over the rainbow." Such Edens are representations of a dreamed-of place where people live together peacefully without pain or death or broken hearts. But in literature as in life, we quickly discover that Eden is gone. That secret garden we thought would be a place of perfect rest and happiness is not to be found this side of eternity.

The Garden of Eden, for that matter, never survived the first generation of the human race. After that initial act of treason against God, Eden's hours were numbered.

Whatever consequences Adam and Eve expected as a result of their first sin, three changes came immediately in the Garden of Eden—fear, guilt, and blame. That very evening, when God came for His late afternoon visit, Adam and Eve were not waiting for Him at the gate as they had done before. When God called out, "Adam, where are you?" the first guilty sinner came from his hiding place and said, "I heard You in the garden, and I was afraid because I was naked; so I hid."

God replied, "Who told you that you were naked? Have you eaten of the tree that I commanded you not to eat from?"

Perhaps Adam and Eve had already discussed what they had done and who was to blame. Their accusations certainly seem to have been well rehearsed:

"And the man said, 'The woman You put here with me—she gave me some fruit from the tree and I ate it.' "

"Then the Lord God said to the woman, 'What is this you have done?' The woman said, 'The serpent deceived me, and I ate.' " (See Genesis 3.)

Does it seem that Adam's assigning of blame touched not only Eve but perhaps even God Himself, when he said,

"The woman *You* put here with me. . ."? And how quickly Eve followed after with her own accusations to make sure she was not left holding the bag!

Throughout the centuries, the human race, individually and collectively, has developed great skill in hoisting on everyone else the responsibility for all the bad and difficult things that have happened in our lives—our own sins and bad choices, the tragedies of nature, the unspeakable evils of the world, as well as the normal inconveniences and mistakes that are a part of human society.

The fact we all have to face sooner or later is that *we are all guilty*; we have all contributed to the destruction of Eden.

But what if the distinctions between the guilty party and the injured party are clear and well-defined? What does a person do when physical or emotional or spiritual pain has been unfairly inflicted, perhaps repeatedly? How can we make sense out of a world that is not "fair"? A world in which people in power or authority hurt people they ought to protect? What about:

> The woman whose marriage has been damaged because of the sexual abuse perpetrated by someone she should have been able to trust as a child?

> The man who has spent his entire life trying to earn the love and approval of a father he could never please?

> The teenage girl feeling rejected by an ambitious mother, because she is not the school beauty, the cheerleading captain, the prom queen?

> The pastor whose ministry has been damaged by the cruel gossip of church members who are spiteful and mean?

The troubled woman whose best friend traitorously revealed her darkest secrets to other people in the church and community?

The wife whose husband carried on an affair, even while he kept up an appearance of faithfulness and godliness?

The wife who for years hid the marks of her husband's repeated violence, even while he maintained a position of honor in his community?

How *can* we ever forgive the hurts inflicted by people we have loved and trusted? Why, in fact, *should* we let someone off the hook who has done us wrong?

THREE FACTS OF LIFE

None of life makes sense apart from our understanding of how God fits into the picture. Here are the facts we have to consider:

1. We cannot avoid the truth that we live in a world deeply damaged by sin. With the introduction of evil, Paradise was lost. Sin permeated every good thing God had made—the human personality, the body, and the mind. All human relationships were tainted. Nature itself groans under the heavy consequences of sin and daily reveals the scars of sin. God in His infinite wisdom, and in His great capacity to turn the greatest evil into something that will bring glory to Himself, has allowed the prince of this world—Satan himself—to hurt and to spoil and to destroy for a time.

For this reason, we should look at everything that happens to us as coming from a primary source. People may, in their selfishness or hate, do us wrong. Satan may even deliberately design a great sorrow to destroy our faith. Still, back of everything painful, behind every disappointment, is a God who has allowed evil to exist. Though He gives us freedom of choice—even to make bad choices— He does *not* allow His plans and designs to be thwarted. He is not inept, unconcerned, or out to lunch. The evil intentions of people do not take God by surprise. What He has permitted in your experience or mine, He has planned as a way to complete His good purposes in our lives.

Of course, it doesn't make sense to us! How could it, in the light of our inability to see the future, or even to understand the past or present?

Long ago God had to remind the Children of Israel, in the middle of their great perplexity and sorrow, that He was wiser than they. " 'For My thoughts are not your thoughts, neither are your ways My ways,' " declares the Lord. " 'As the heavens are higher than the earth, so are My ways higher than your ways and My thoughts than your thoughts' " (Isaiah 55:8-9).

Until we acknowledge that God could have stopped the very thing that hurt us, but chose not to out of His superior justice and knowledge and love, then nothing in life is going to make sense.

Imagine the faith that was required of Job, who at the touch of Satan lost everything, and still was able to say about God, "If I go to the east, He is not there; if I go to the west, I do not find Him. When He is at work in the north, I do not see Him; when He turns to the south, I catch no glimpse of Him. But He knows the way that I take; when He has tested me, I will come forth as gold" (Job 23:8-10).

2. Sin is terrible beyond belief; sin is universal; sin requires forgiveness. In the process of forgiving the sin of one who has hurt us, we do not have to deny the awfulness of the sin. What we *do* have to acknowledge is that in God's eyes there are not degrees of sin. Perhaps adultery and murder have more serious consequences in society, but they are not "worse" sins than pride or lying or selfishness. They all have to be cured in the same way. Every sin any of us commits is a slap in the face of God and

comes from a heart that is damaged by evil beyond all human comprehension. Jeremiah 17:9 says bluntly, "The heart is deceitful above all things and beyond cure. Who can understand it?"

3. Fortunately, we are not bleakly trapped in the web of our own failure, nor are we hopeless victims of the sins and failures of others. Flawed by inherited sin and by the sins of our own choice, living in a world without peace, with disease and decay and death as predictable as the rising sun, we have something better than the original Eden! When we have been redeemed by the blood of Jesus Christ, made children and heirs, then we have the moment-by-moment presence of God dwelling within our very being. Unlike Adam and Eve who moved in and out of the presence of God in the Garden of Eden, we are never left alone; we never have to make a single decision without the direction of His Spirit, if we choose to listen to Him.

Unlike Adam and Eve, we also have the Word of God to study and to bury deep within our hearts. We do not have to "remember" what God said; we can go straight back to the source for instant confirmation!

THE RICHNESS OF GOD'S GRACE

Best of all, we who have sinned and have been sinned against have learned something about the grace of God, an attribute always present in the character of God, but probably never understood or revealed until the loss of Eden. If we, along with Adam and Eve, had not been removed from the blessings of an earthly Eden, we would never have understood the depths of our sin or the inexpressible love of God: "Where sin increased, grace increased all the more" (Romans 5:20).

Arthur W. Pink explains it like this:

> God alone is able to bring good out of evil and make
> even the wrath of man to praise Him. The Fall has

*afforded Him an opportunity to exhibit His wisdom
and display the riches of His grace to an extent
which, so far as we can see, He never could have
done, had not sin entered the world. In the sphere of
redemption Christ has not only reversed the effect of
the Fall, but because of it has brought in a better
thing. If God could have found a way, consistent with
His own character, to restore man to the position
which he occupied before he became a transgressor,
it would have been a remarkable triumph; but that
through Christ man should actually be the gainer is
a transcendent miracle of Divine wisdom and grace.
Yet such is the case. The redeemed have gained more
through the last Adam than they lost through the first
Adam. They occupy a more exalted position. Before
the Fall Adam dwelt in an earthly Paradise, but the
redeemed have been made to sit with Christ in heavenly places. Through redemption they have been
blest with a nobler nature. Before the Fall man possessed a natural life; but now, all in Christ have been
made partakers of the Divine nature. They have ob-
tained a new standing before God. Adam was merely
innocent, which is a negative condition, but believers
in Christ are righteous, which is a positive state. We
share a better inheritance. Adam was lord of Eden,
but believers are "heirs of all things," "heirs of God
and joint heirs with Christ." Through grace we have
been made capable of a deeper joy than unfallen
spirits have known: the bliss of pardoned sin, the
heaven of deep conscious obligation to Divine mercy.
In Christ believers enjoy a closer relationship to God
than was possible before the Fall. Adam was merely
a creature, but we are members of the body of
Christ . . . "members of His body, of His flesh and of
His bones." How marvelous! We have been taken into
union with Deity itself, so that the Son of God is not
ashamed to call us brethren. The Fall provided the*

need of Redemption, and through the redeeming work
of the Cross, believers have a portion which unfallen
Adam could never have attained unto. Truly, "where
sin abounded, grace did much more abound." [1]

And then we have the promise of Eden restored. In this truly happy ending, better than any fairy tale, better than the best Utopia invented by the human mind, there is heaven. What comforting words the Lord Jesus left with His disciples (and with us) when He said:

Do not let your hearts be troubled. Trust in God; trust
also in Me. In My Father's house are many rooms; if it
were not so, I would have told you. I am going there to
prepare a place for you. And if I go and prepare a place
for you, I will come back and take you to be with Me
that you also may be where I am (John 14:1-3).

Revelation 21:3-4 adds this further description of what our restored Eden will be like:

Now the dwelling of God is with men, and He will live
with them. They will be His people, and God Himself
will be with them and be their God. He will wipe
every tear from their eyes. There will be no more
death or mourning or crying or pain, for the old order
of things has passed away.

How much clearer our perspective would be on our own failings, and the failings of others, if we could see the conclusions to life as God sees them. How much easier forgiveness would be, if we had the power to grasp the awesome depth of the grace of God!

There is a point at which all of us who have been hurt—whether by our own sins or the sins of others—must accept the fact that this side of heaven, humanity will always behave like humanity. God did not promise us that *our* forgiveness or *our* love would be great enough to transform ourselves or others into creatures who would not have to deal with a fallen nature and predisposition to evil. We must come to the place of doing what we do because of our faith in the One who is refining and polishing His own, and preparing them for an eternity where "the old order of things has passed away."

TWO

WHY FORGIVENESS IS SO HARD

E lise was a young woman who had been hurt by the repeated unfaithfulness of her husband. He claimed to be a Christian and Elise believed this to be true. He seemed to be genuinely heartbroken over his sin and willingly agreed to lengthy counseling. He took every step the counselor suggested, building toward healing and restoration, and he assured Elise that he loved her.

The Christian psychologist Elise talked to briefly told her that she had biblical grounds for a divorce if she decided to go that route, but she loved her husband and did not want her young children to be hurt by divorce. She chose to forgive.

Bob's involvement with other women had been expensive and the process of rebuilding the marriage had required great self-sacrifice on Elise's part. First Bob lost his job because his affair with a coworker was revealed to the president of the company where he worked. Elise had to be the sole support of the family for a time. Then there was an expensive move to another city to get a new start at a lesser-paying job for Bob. Also, at Elise's insistence Bob had numerous sessions with a counselor who helped him trace the early damage in his life that made him particularly vulnerable to sexual sin.

Gradually Bob and Elise worked through the repairs and the rebuilding process in their marriage and became actively involved in a church where they developed a ministry with other hurting couples.

One day, in the process of counseling another young woman whose husband had been unfaithful, sudden past memories overwhelmed Elise and she drifted into depression. It was a distressing time for her and for the rest of her family as well. As she remembered the pain of her own past heartache, she began probing old wounds.

Bob was frustrated. "How can you keep digging up the past?" he asked. "I thought you said you had forgiven the things I did, but evidently that isn't entirely true. Can't you see I've done everything in my power to make things right?"

"I know that," Elise countered with tears. "But suddenly it doesn't seem fair. We've paid thousands of dollars for your healing, but I still hurt. I've worked hard, made adjustments, and tried to let go of the past, but somehow the pain just doesn't go away!"

This explosion was all the more confusing and disturbing, since it was totally contradictory to Elise's usual gentle way of meeting problems.

Eventually, Elise was able to see that her depression came out of the wrong expectations about what forgiveness could do. She had secretly believed that if she did all the right things when Bob sinned, she could somehow "erase" that painful passage in her life and go back to what she assumed life was "supposed" to be. She wanted to reconstruct her childhood dream of a "perfect" marriage—one which did not require the repeated process of forgiving, dealing with the consequences of sin, and the loss of innocence that goes with growing up.

She discovered that forgiveness is not a "natural" process. It is difficult, often progressive, and demands grace and power beyond what most of us consider to be possible.

WHY FORGIVENESS IS SO HARD   23

PERPLEXING RELATIONSHIPS

The business of forgiveness is rarely a simple transaction between the injured and the one who caused the injury. All our relationships are complicated by other relationships, by the memories each of us carries from our past, by our own perfectionism or lack of it, by our perceptions of gender—"You can never trust men; they always look out for themselves first!"—or by race or class or "whatever."

Think about King David's perplexing relationships with his children. First, we have Amnon, oldest son and presumed heir to the throne, who raped his half-sister, Tamar. David knew the Old Testament law: a demand for the death penalty when an engaged or married woman was raped. The rape of a sister by her brother required a public execution. "He has dishonored his sister and will be held responsible" (Leviticus 20:17). David did not demand the death penalty for Amnon. That part of the story concludes with only this simple statement, "But when King David heard all of these things, he was furious."

What was David thinking? Why didn't he *do something*? Could it be that he remembered with great shame his own adultery and therefore could not bring himself to deal with Amnon's sin because of his own guilt? Was he reluctant to expose the sin publicly and sully the reputation of the heir to the throne?

Absalom, Tamar's full brother, waited two years to see what the king would do; then he took matters into his own hand and carefully engineered the death of Amnon. Whatever risks were involved, Absalom decided to force the king's hand. Perhaps, after seeing that David had done nothing to punish Amnon, Absalom may have hoped David's anger would quickly cool.

After Absalom fled and remained out of the country for three years, David still did nothing. But 2 Samuel 13:39 says, "And the spirit of the king longed to go to Absalom, for he was consoled concerning Amnon's death."

Still, David did nothing to show his forgiveness! Absalom remained in Geshur, a banished prince!

Here was a man with two sons who had committed violent crimes, and neither one had paid the legal penalty involved. We almost get the impression that now they were both forgiven—Amnon posthumously and Absalom exiled in a far country. Well . . . *almost* forgiven! As much as David longed for the presence of this vanished son, he would not say the words to bring him back home!

Eventually, through a rather dangerous object lesson staged by Absalom, David did agree to let him return. It looked as though forgiveness was finally going to be complete.

Wrong! When Absalom arrived in Jerusalem David sent word, "He must go to his own house; he must not see my face."

How dangerous incomplete forgiveness is! Absalom, with all the gifts and capabilities of his father, grew more bitter day by day. Eventually he attempted to seize the kingdom from the aging King David and was slaughtered in the process.

Of course, we have no guarantee that the story would have ended differently, had David been able to deal with his sons' behavior, either in punishment or forgiveness. Still, it is logical to assume that Absalom's bitterness and loneliness provided the fertile ground for the uprising of son against father.

As concise as this account in the life of David happens to be, the emotional impact of his grief at the death of Absalom almost pours from the pages of Scripture, "O my son Absalom! My son, my son Absalom! If only I had died instead of you—O Absalom, my son, my son!" (2 Samuel 18:33)

Was David's great grief partly a reflection of his own unfinished business? We are tempted to speculate how different the ending to the story might have been had David's forgiveness of Absalom been complete.

Why is it that you and I, like David, have such a hard time forgiving someone who has hurt us?

WHY FORGIVENESS IS SO HARD

1. Forgiveness is hard because it takes away the tool that allows us to punish one who has hurt us. If I refuse to forgive someone, then I get to "play God"—to cause the offender equal pain by my anger and by my refusal to heal the relationship. It empowers me to make someone else suffer as I feel I have suffered.

However, when we use unforgiveness as a way of getting vengeance, we are stepping over into territory God has reserved for Himself alone. Romans 12:19 says, "Do not take revenge, my friends, but leave room for God's wrath, for it is written: 'It is Mine to avenge; I will repay,' says the Lord."

If I attempt to take over what is God's responsibility, I am apt to jeopardize the timing of God's discipline in the life of the one I want to punish, as well as God's best plan and purposes for my own life. As David Seamands says:

> The idea that fear and guilt and self-condemnation will keep us from sinning and therefore give us inner peace and joy is completely contrary to experience. Those who live that way are filled with inner turmoil and driven by strong—even strange, and seemingly uncontrollable—compulsions towards the very sins they try the hardest to avoid.[1]

How foolish we would be to try to force anyone who has hurt us into that position! We do not further the work of the Holy Spirit if we try to induce guilt and fear in that one who has done wrong.

2. Forgiveness is hard, because in forgiving we may put ourselves in the place of being hurt again. Especially in close relationships, when we have been offended, we tend

to think we can control the other person if we make it obvious we are holding on to our anger and pain. It is easy to believe that our anger and unforgiveness will keep the offender in line—make him behave!

But it just doesn't work that way! Proverbs 16:6 says, "Through love and faithfulness sin is atoned for; through the fear of the Lord a man avoids evil." It was not God's wrath and vengeance against you and me that made it possible for us to come to a point of repentance and faith in Jesus Christ. It was His great mercy!

Romans 2:4 warns us, "Do you show contempt for the riches of His kindness, tolerance and patience, not realizing that God's kindness leads you toward repentance?"

If mercy and kindness are the keys to repentance toward God, surely there is a principle here that works in human relationships as well.

In 1991 Jewish Cantor Michael Weisser and his wife began to receive threatening telephone calls from Larry Trapp, a Ku Klux Klan recruiter. In a remarkable display of forgiveness, they decided to visit this former grand dragon of the White Knights of the Ku Klux Klan in his own home. They found him to be a blind paraplegic diabetic, bitter and angry and gravely ill.

First they invited him to have dinner in their home, at which time they spent hours in conversation with him. Eventually Trapp moved in with the couple and their two teenage children; he lived with them until his death ten months later. During his stay at the home of the very people he had persecuted, Trapp publicly recanted his relationship with the Klan. On one occasion he sent flowers to Mrs. Weisser with the note, "Thanks for changing me from a dragon to a butterfly."[2]

At Larry Trapp's funeral, others who mourned along with the Weissers had also been persecuted by Trapp's harassing phone calls. What had begun as a campaign of hate was turned by forgiveness into a beautiful demonstration of love and mercy!

We cannot *make* people be good. Only God can do that! But we *can* build the kind of environment of love that allows room for God to work!

3. Forgiveness is hard because it demands a long, hard look at our own failure and sin. When we are absolutely honest with ourselves, we have to acknowledge that forgiveness is necessary and possible not because we are so "right" ourselves, but because *we* require the same kind of forgiveness from God who sees the deepest recesses of *our* hearts and knows thoroughly *our* own failures and sins. No wonder we prefer staying at the "anger" level; it is so much safer than dealing with ourselves and our own hearts.

How wise we would be to daily repeat the prayer of David, "Search me, O God, and know my heart; test me and know my anxious thoughts. See if there is any offensive way in me, and lead me in the way everlasting" (Psalm 139:23-24).

4. Forgiveness is hard because it is so closely linked to our submission to God and to others. When I forgive, I not only lose my power to punish and control, but I also forfeit my "rights" to wallow in my pain, to bolster my wounded pride, and to display my spiritual authority.

Forgiveness intensifies the need for humility, not only on the part of the offender but for the victim as well. Forgiveness says, "I forgive you because that frees me to deal with my own sin and failure."

A lack of forgiveness always reveals flaws and weaknesses in our own spiritual fabric:

Inflexibility—an inability to change our perceptions and our position in relationship to others;

Cowardice—a fear of giving up our power; a reluctance to give the one who has hurt us "another chance";

Pride—a determination to maintain our cover of "righteousness' in the face of someone else's sinfulness";

Insensitivity—a callousness in viewing the problem, a refusal to acknowledge the conditions and temptations that precipitated the offense, a lack of awareness of the deepest needs of the one who has hurt us;

Lack of spiritual maturity — a spiritual problem. "For if you forgive men when they sin against you, your heavenly Father will also forgive you. But if you do not forgive men their sins, your Father will not forgive your sins" (Matthew 6:14-15).

Genuine forgiveness involves a transaction with God Himself. If we are to have a relationship with Him, then we will need to practice His forgiveness in our relationships with others. Our happiness, our future, and the blessing of God itself is dependent upon our willingness to be obedient in this matter.

Whatever relationship we hope to have with God is irrevocably linked with this matter of forgiveness. We cannot bypass the necessity for forgiveness in the eyes of God by a lifetime of good works or by a multitude of gifts we bring to Him — our money, our service, or even our praise. We must begin at the point where God began with us — forgiveness.

In his famous little book, *The Imitation of Christ*, Thomas á Kempis speaks for God, "My son, do not take it to heart, if you see others honored and promoted, but yourself despised and humiliated. Lift up your heart to me in heaven, and do not grieve because men despise you on earth."[3]

At the heart of all unforgiveness lies the pain of lost honor. We may be able to forgive the pain the offender has caused, but we cannot forgive the humiliation that comes with knowing this one did not value us enough to avoid hurting us. Only as we are able to see our value to God will the dishonor of human thoughtlessness become insignificant.

THREE

WHY WE ABSOLUTELY MUST FORGIVE

I am a collector, but a rather indiscriminate one. My home reflects my fascination with groups of related objects—miniature tea sets, unusual musical instruments and miniature houses. I love noticing the various expressions of design by artists of all ages and cultures in their creation of a particular similar object. If I am not careful, I will find myself getting involved in other people's collections as well, and spending money for frivolities they don't even want!

However, it isn't just objects I collect; I am a great one for collecting lists, and I am apt to file away all sorts of charming little bits of information simply because I find them interesting. Even though I may not be able to remember an important person's name in the middle of an introduction, I can easily reel off my mental list of every teacher I ever had from first grade through college, and I could probably name at least ten of my classmates from my sixth grade class at Longfellow Elementary School!

Well, so far, so good. But then, through the circumstances of one difficult year, I finally had to acknowledge that I also had a major collection of bad memories that had to be discarded. After years of rearing my own children, writing books and articles for women, teaching high school and college students, and ministering to women in the church and in various seminars, I found this a difficult admission to make. I had accumulated a lifetime of unfinished business—a collection of memories that hurt or angered me because I had never really forgiven those who had inflicted the pain.

It wasn't that I was sitting around feeling sorry for myself! Nor was the issue a problem of not loving the Lord and desiring to serve Him with all my heart. I longed for God to use me; I really wanted to glorify His name.

HINDRANCES TO FORGIVING

The problem came because I did not understand how to deal with the things that "went wrong" in my life.

My first assumption was that bad things do not happen to good people. Therefore, if something hurt me, it was because I was not doing the right things. If I could just work a little harder serving the Lord, reading my Bible and meeting the needs of other people, I would not be hurt by pain or the difficulties of living in a damaged world.

My second assumption was that it is always wrong to be angry. If someone did wrong or took advantage of me or otherwise caused me pain, I was supposed to "forgive and forget" and simply pretend the hurt had not happened. I believed that "dying to self" meant never challenging wrong or expressing pain over things that had hurt. It wasn't until I had acknowledged a lifetime tendency toward depression—not clinical or totally debilitating, but nevertheless, real—that I began to see its relationship to unexpressed anger.

My third assumption was that knowing the Word of God and being able to explain it effectively to myself and other people meant that I would not have to struggle with the same kinds of temptations and problems that plague those who do not know the Word or choose to live by it.

My fourth assumption had to do with my own strong penchant for "doing things right"—a belief that my unidentified perfectionism was a virtue! Since *I* was trying so hard to be perfect, I couldn't understand why other people did not try to do the same! I felt irritation and some bitterness at people who did not think as I did. I found that I was frequently frustrated with those who were late or lazy or messy or who failed to "play by the rules."

What I finally had to deal with was the fact that although I "loved" many people, I was accumulating a wide assortment of grievances in the vault of my memory. I would have said that I loved them "in spite of" the things they did, and that the problems I saw "didn't matter" in our relationship. But unconsciously, the ledger was filling up with accusations against the human race in general and specific people in particular. These accusations proved, "You really can't trust anybody. Sooner or later the people you love and trust the most will let you down."

I finally had to admit that my frequent feelings of restlessness and depression had to do with a lifetime of suppressing anger and frustration. I had never learned to track unforgiveness to its source and deal with it.

Plainly and simply, I was going to have to learn how to forgive. But forgive what?

I needed to learn how to forgive people for being human—for having unmet needs of their own, for being flawed by sin and by circumstance, for being unable to meet all my needs.

I needed to learn to forgive people for being "different"—for viewing life in an opposite way from my own vision, for having a differing set of values, for choosing their own lifestyle even if it did not agree with mine, and for being irritatingly and confusingly their own selves!

I needed to learn how to forgive specific, identifiable sins committed by others, to acknowledge them and name them if they were sins that had hurt me, and then to let them go.

I needed to learn how to forgive myself—to see myself in the light of God's love and forgiveness.

I even needed to learn how to "forgive" God for the things He had allowed in my life. Now, obviously, God is perfectly righteous and holy and fair, and He does not require forgiveness from anybody. But those of us struggling with perplexing pain and terrible sorrow do have to come to a point of recognizing God's right to *be* God, whether or not we understand all that is involved.

WHY FORGIVING IS ABSOLUTELY ESSENTIAL

1. We must forgive others, because a failure to do so will destroy us. Our emotional balance, our perceptions of life and other people, and our capacity to make rational judgments are all affected by our ability to forgive.

> *Anyone who claims to be in the light but hates his brother is still in the darkness. Whoever loves his brother lives in the light, and there is nothing in him to make him stumble. But whoever hates his brother is in the darkness and walks around in the darkness; he does not know where he is going, because the darkness has blinded him (1 John 2:9-11).*

What is the result of unforgiveness, of hatred when we have been hurt? Blindness, a loss of direction, a loss of purpose.

We are all constantly reminded of the dangers of addictions—to drugs, to food, to gambling, to alcohol, to smoking, to pornography or to sex. What we probably do not acknowledge is that it is possible for a person to become addicted to anger, to unforgiveness. In fact, you might say that bitterness *is* an addiction to anger. In describing the seven deadly sins, Frederick Buechner talks about the pleasure of savoring "the last toothsome morsel of both the pain you are giving and the pain you are getting back" when you refuse to forgive. But in the end, Buechner says, "What you are wolfing down is yourself."[1]

Bitterness, like all addictions, is self-destructing. It sacrifices all that is good and precious, all that is positive and eternal, for the momentary satisfaction of feeding one's own executioner.

2. Failure to forgive spoils all relationships. "Make every effort to live in peace with all men and to be holy; without holiness no one will see the Lord. See to it that no one misses the grace of God and that no bitter root grows up to cause trouble and defile many" (Hebrews 12:14-15).

People living in rural areas of the South quickly learn to identify kudzu, an attractive groundcover which was brought over from Japan a number of years ago to help control erosion. Kudzu grows quickly and soon covers everything in its territory with a lush blanket of green. It hides the eyesores of nature and the refuse of modern society. Unfortunately, it does more than that. When left to itself it can obliterate an entire forest, cover large buildings with a ghostly coat of green, and ruin crops. It is almost impossible to control or to destroy.

Bitterness and unforgiveness are rather like kudzu. They seem to satisfy justice, to alleviate the pain that results from someone else's thoughtlessness or evil intent. The problem is that they go beyond the culprit, the perpetrator of pain, and invade the lives of innocent people who had nothing to do with the pain inflicted.

A large family of adult siblings had difficulty deciding what to do after their father became gravely ill. The mother had been dead for a number of years and the children bore the emotional and financial responsibility for their ailing father. All the life support systems available had been used, but the doctor declared that their beloved father was medically brain dead. Though keeping him on a life support system might sustain the basic necessities of survival, he would never again be conscious. The family would have to decide what to do.

There was immediate disagreement. Some in the family felt that life lived under any condition is so precious that the father should be kept alive at any cost. Other members of the family argued that the father himself would not choose to live under these circumstances, and that maintaining a life support system indefinitely would not only use all the family's present financial resources, but would create a heavy indebtedness for years to come.

Eventually, the family agreed to vote on what should be done, with the understanding that all of the family would submit to a majority vote. When the discussions were over and the vote was taken, the majority ruled that the plug should be pulled; the father's life should not be artificially sustained. The doctor was informed; the papers were signed; the machines were turned off. In a matter of minutes the father ceased to breathe and the doctor pronounced him dead.

But from that moment a quarrel began that contaminated three generations of the family—between those who chose to "murder father" and those who did not. What had started out as a democratic, seemingly logical decision turned into years of bitterness. Every element of consideration was lost in the unforgiven, unforgotten decision that had been made that fateful day.

3. Failure to forgive will have its effect on the health and well-being of the one who does not forgive. There is a sense of unacknowledged worthlessness and condemnation that comes with unforgiveness: GUILT!

When our children were young, we had a pet poodle, Tomte, who frequently got into trouble by her curious investigating. We once had to have a fishhook removed from her lip when she got into fishing gear, and we often had to rescue her from confining places where she explored.

During her first Christmas season, the family came home from a shopping trip only to discover Tomte had torn from the tree as many little candy bells as she could reach. The floor was covered with bits of aluminum foil and numerous chocolate bells showing the marks of her teeth.

"You bad, bad dog!" the children said. "Look what

you've done! That candy is going to make you sick." We all added our angry comments.

Tomte dropped her head and slunk away to her bed. And sure enough, she *was* sick, very sick, until we began to be concerned about her health.

"I'll bet she has eaten too much of that aluminum foil and poisoned herself," one family member said. "Maybe she ate more chocolate than we knew," said another. "I think we should take her to the vet."

And so that is exactly what we did. The doctor checked her over carefully and then laughed. "There's not a thing wrong with this dog except a guilty conscience! She knows you are mad at her for tearing up the Christmas tree!"

Of course, people are not dogs, and it is important not to make quick generalizations about the relationships between people and guilt. Still, it is true that guilt does produce stress, and stress which is not released in some healthy way can cause physical ailments.

A Chattanooga cardiologist once said, "I could empty 90 percent of the beds in the hospital where I work if I could cure the problems of the heart."

It would be arrogant for any of us to assume we know the sources of someone else's illness; but we can, if we carefully examine our own hearts, often trace our physical and emotional stresses back to those places where we feel ourselves to be guilty and judged.

But whether or not we feel guilty when we fail to forgive, there is one who sees our unforgiving heart and takes account. "Don't grumble against each other, brothers, or you will be judged. The Judge is standing at the door!" (James 5:9)

God does not regard forgiveness as optional. If we allow our grudges to accumulate, the God of heaven sees and is grieved; He judges what we do. The judgment may not come like a bolt of lightning from heaven, but it will come—perhaps in our health, in disappointed dreams or in other failed relationships.

Unforgiveness will destroy us.

4. Failure to forgive casts doubt on our relationship with the Lord. "If anyone says, 'I love God,' yet hates his brother, he is a liar. For anyone who does not love his brother, whom he has seen, cannot love God, whom he has not seen. And He has given us this command: Whoever loves God must also love his brother" (1 John 4:20-21).

I suspect that many of us who consider ourselves loving people may have to question whether our lack of forgiveness in a specific instance actually reflects upon the character and quality of our love in general. Is not our unforgiveness of someone we have seen and perhaps had close contact with a direct act of disobedience against the One who commanded us to forgive? Dare we claim we love God while we disobey Him?

When I forgive one who has hurt me, I am expressing not only my love for God, but my faith in His ability to change people I cannot change.

In *Dancing with Porcupines*, Bob Phillips writes:

> *When we try to change another person from the outside, we tend to destroy that person. We need to accept people . . . the way they are. That's what Jesus did. And if there is negative behavior which needs to be changed—and we all have some—we need to allow God to change [that person] . . . from the inside out. Sometimes we usurp the responsibility of being the change agent which rightfully belongs to the Holy Spirit. Instead, we need to relax and trust that God is in control.*[2]

We must deal with other people's sins as we would want ours dealt with. In Luke 6:37-38 we read:

> *Do not judge, and you will not be judged. Do not condemn, and you will not be condemned. Forgive, and you will be forgiven. Give, and it will be given to*

you. A good measure, pressed down, shaken together
and running over, will be poured into your lap. For
with the measure you use, it will be measured to you.

When we see what other people do to us, we know only what is happening on the outside, and so we judge them and their responses to us on the basis of externals.

But when we judge ourselves, we view our own responses by all the extenuating circumstances we never allow others. We *know* what pressures provoked our cruel words, our selfish reactions. We measure with a rubber ruler. We do not allow other people the same standards.

Assuming that you have been hurt, you may have to remember that people who hurt others have themselves been hurt. It is true that we are each responsible for the decisions we make; our capacity to forgive will increase if we humbly identify our own vulnerability and measure out to others the same kind of forgiveness we would want for ourselves.

FOUR

WHEN
CONFRONTATION
IS IN ORDER

C harles would have called himself a pillar of the church. While he was a deacon, he challenged the church policy of allowing divorced people to sing in the choir: when no one would listen to him, he got angry and resigned. The people never asked him to serve again.

Charles considered himself a kind of spiritual "watchdog" and he made it his business to confront sin and failure wherever he saw it. The youth pastor shuddered when he saw Charles coming, and the women of the church nervously adjusted hair and clothing anytime he walked into the room. Sometimes the teenagers snickered and whispered, "Here come da judge!"

One day he discovered his teenage daughter was pregnant. He was alternately furious and devastated. How *dare* she ruin his reputation! When he threatened to throw her out of the house, the pastor interceded and the church rallied to give her support and healing.

Eventually, Charles saw that his kind of confrontation had been neither biblical nor helpful. He had assumed that his "watchdogging" would be a spiritual protection — not only for the church people but also for his own family. God used the problem in his home to teach Charles what biblical confrontation is and what it is not.

WHAT CONFRONTATION IS NOT

Just saying the word "confrontation" conveys an image of one standing with elbows out, fists clenched, eyes blazing. In fact, the Latin word *confrontare* suggests a picture of two people facing each other over a common wall, with foreheads pressed together in anger.

While confrontation may indeed involve hostility or defiance, *The American Heritage Dictionary of the English Language* states that it also means, "to bring close together for comparison or examination." Biblical confrontation, when sin is discovered, fits that definition exactly.

1. Confrontation is not the same thing as judging. The Scripture makes it clear that we do not have the right to judge, that is, to pass sentence or to condemn, one who has done wrong. That is God's responsibility, and He does not take lightly our usurping of His authority. In Matthew 7:1-5 we read:

> *Do not judge, or you too will be judged. For in the same way you judge others, you will be judged, and with the measure you use, it will be measured to you.*
>
> *Why do you look at the speck of sawdust in your brother's eye and pay no attention to the plank in your own eye? How can you say to your brother, "Let me take the speck out of your eye," when all the time there is a plank in your own eye? You hypocrite, first take the plank out of your own eye, and then you will see clearly to remove the speck from your brother's eye.*

In her book *From Frustration to Freedom,* Karen Dockrey gives five reasons why my judging of others is dangerous:

I am not qualified.

I tend to use it to show my superiority.

My judgment can be the opposite of kindness, tolerance, and patience.

My judgment may be more for my convenience than to draw persons toward repentance.

Judgment is God's job.[1]

2. Confrontation is not the same thing as venting anger. In fact, if confrontation is to be handled in the way that God demands, it requires us to deal with our anger first.

In the revelation of some wrong that has been perpetrated against us, our first reactions are not necessarily bad. Ephesians 4:26 says, "In your anger do not sin." The problem is that we often want to hold anger to ourselves just a little while longer, to lick it like an all-day sucker! The same verse gives a good boundary or deadline for settling the unfinished business of our anger, "Do not let the sun go down while you are still angry."

To be truly obedient to the Word of God, we may have to consciously, deliberately, and prayerfully set aside enough time to be able to let go of our anger. There is a sense in which giving up our anger—even when confrontation has not taken place and when we have no guarantee that there will be restoration—is a matter of faith. We may have to spiritually and emotionally dump all our grievances and the accompanying anger in the hands of the Lord Jesus, and consciously commit ourselves to claiming His peace, *even before we know how it will all turn out.* It is only in making the problem God's problem, instead of our own, that we will be able to relinquish our anger.

Ephesians 4:29-32 gives us detailed instructions for dealing with our anger:

> *Do not let any unwholesome talk come out of your mouths, but only what is helpful for building others up according to their needs, that it may benefit those who listen. And do not grieve the Holy Spirit of God, with whom you were sealed for the day of redemption. Get rid of all bitterness, rage and anger, brawl-*

ing and slander, along with every form of malice. Be
kind and compassionate to one another, forgiving
each other, just as in Christ God forgave you.

In this passage we see five ways anger may be expressed, all of which are unhealthy:

Bitterness: anger turned inward, "anger gone to
   seed."
Rage: anger out of control.
Brawling: anger turned to violence.
Slander: anger seeking revenge through whispers
   and innuendos.
Malice: anger plotting vengeance and evil.

We cannot begin to work on the problem in the life of the one who has offended us until we have settled the problem of our own anger.

3. Confrontation is not contradictory to the biblical rules of submission and authority. Sometimes a person who has been abused by an individual in a place of authority wrongly assumes he or she has no right to challenge that person's sin. How often evil deeds have been covered and continue to harm others because of this mistaken view of authority!

David Seamands discusses the problem that faces so many damaged Christians—particularly those who have been abused:

They would rather take all the blame for what some-
one did to them than face the truth about the persons
who did it. This is especially true when the victimiz-
ers are people they want to love and respect—like
parents, important relatives, teachers, preachers, or
spouses.
   A vicious and nearly unbreakable circle of guilt is
set up when we hold to that guilt. There seems no

way out, because there's no way for God's grace to
get in. His grace enters only when we forgive those
who have sinned against us. And we can't really for-
give them until we admit how much they've hurt us,
and then face how we feel toward them. And that's
impossible as long as we keep on taking responsibil-
ity for the sins they have committed.[2]

James 5:19-20 tells us, "My brothers, if one of you
should wander from the truth and someone should bring
him back, remember this: Whoever turns a sinner from
the error of his way will save him from death and cover
over a multitude of sins."

Someone who continually does wrong without challenge—even though a child of God—puts himself in the
place of God's direst punishment, perhaps even death. If
we love those who are in the body of Christ, then we will
do whatever is in our power to keep that from happening.

Then what *should* be our response when we are damaged by another's sins?

We certainly are not to simply grin and bear it, particularly if physical, sexual, or emotional abuse is involved.
Acts of crime or violence can never be ignored or excused!

Confrontation will involve naming the offense, expressing the hurt involved, and working out a plan that will
help to bring changes.

Second Timothy 2:23-26 tells us what kind of attitude is
required for confrontation:

Don't have anything to do with foolish and stupid
arguments, because you know they produce quar-
rels. And the Lord's servant must not quarrel; in-
stead, he must be kind to everyone, able to teach, not
resentful. Those who oppose him he must gently in-
struct, in the hope that God will grant them repen-
tance leading them to a knowledge of the truth, and
that they will come to their senses and escape from

*the trap of the devil, who has taken them captive to
do his will.*

Notice the biblical rules of person-to-person confrontation: not fighting; staying gentle; instructing in patience those who oppose; working toward restoration.

This is the same plan for confrontation that God set up for the Children of Israel in Old Testament law. "Do not hate your brother in your heart. Rebuke your neighbor frankly so you will not share in his guilt. Do not seek revenge or bear a grudge against one of your people, but love your neighbor as yourself. I am the Lord" (Leviticus 19:17-18).

CONFRONTATION IN THE HOME

1. First, if possible, arrange the confrontation to be in private, one on one. This ought to be done kindly and with careful forethought, giving specific examples of continued wrongdoing. It may be necessary to say, "I love you too much to allow you to go on this way without getting help." When a woman is confronting her husband, she may need to add, "I will go with you to get help and I will stand by you as long as you are working on the problem. If you will not go voluntarily to get some spiritual counseling about this problem, then I will go alone. You are too precious and our home is too valuable for us to allow this problem to continue unchallenged."

2. In some cases, confrontation may actually lead to more violence. If a woman knows that this is a possibility, it would be wise for her to seek the help of a trusted advisor to support in the confrontation. She may even require shelter if her life or the lives of her children are in jeopardy.

3. Determine to get counseling for yourself even if your spouse or other family member will not. There are many things you can do to help in a difficult situation.

4. Deal gently with things you don't understand. Unresolved problems in a family are often passed from generation to generation. Even when we confront one who has hurt us deeply, we need to work at understanding the events and conditions that helped to damage the one who has done wrong. Our compassion cannot be a substitute for confrontation; however, it should enable the perpetrator to say, "The buck stops here; I will bring an end to the syndrome of failure in my past."

A PATTERN FOR CONFRONTATION

Brothers, if someone is caught in a sin, you who are spiritual should restore him gently. But watch yourself, or you also may be tempted. Carry each other's burdens, and in this way you will fulfill the law of Christ. If anyone thinks he is something when he is nothing, he deceives himself. Each one should test his own actions. Then he can take pride in himself, without comparing himself to somebody else, for each one should carry his own load (Galatians 6:1-5).

Consider the important principles in this passage:

1. "Caught in a sin," or, as the King James Version puts it, "overtaken in a fault," implies that we might succumb to a particular temptation which we did not expect and were not prepared to face. In judging other people, we should be aware of the difference between a prolonged deliberate act that is wrong, and the failure that comes when one is suddenly tempted to do wrong. This is why it is essential for us to note the warning, "Watch yourself, or you also may be tempted."

2. "You who are spiritual should restore him gently." The prerequisite for biblical restoration is that the "restorer" be spiritual. Larry Crabb says we Christians are more comfortable if we can "classify sin into manageable categories and then scrupulously avoid it." The problem is that

we can identify and classify such sins as murder and adultery and violence, but it is harder to identify covetousness and pride and selfishness. All too often, while we are demanding the correction of the "grosser" sins—even as God requires, we gloss over and minimize our own hard-to-identify sins, for which God also demands repentance.

3. "Carry each other's burdens, and in this way you will fulfill the law of Christ." In the body of Christ, the offender's sins are, in a sense, our sins too. We ought to feel the pain and guilt and isolation that sin brings. This is what "rejoicing with those who rejoice and mourning with those who mourn" is all about (Romans 12:15).

Daniel, that rare biblical saint against whom there is not a single sin recorded, prayed for his sinning brethren as though their sins were his very own:

> O Lord, we and our kings, our princes and our fathers are covered with shame because we have sinned against You. . . . O Lord, listen! O Lord, forgive! O Lord, hear and act! For Your sake, O my God, do not delay, because Your city and Your people bear Your Name (Daniel 9:8, 19).

4. "If anyone thinks he is something when he is nothing, he deceives himself." All of us know of cases in which individuals in places of leadership made accusations against others in places of leadership, and then fell prey to the very sins they had condemned others for committing. It should be a warning for all of us. Not one of us knows how closely we walk to the edge of failure and sin and deep disappointment with ourselves. What a sensitivity we need to develop about our own weaknesses! How wary we should be of our own supposed strengths. "The heart is deceitful above all things and beyond cure," Jeremiah said. "Who can understand it?" (17:9)

5. "Each one should test his own actions. Then he can take pride in himself, without comparing himself to some-

body else, for each one should carry his own load."

We would do well to avoid any comparison of our failures with the failures of others. Just because I have never tasted alcohol, have never smoked a cigarette, does not give me the right to compare myself virtuously with the alcoholic who has been addicted from childhood, or to the smoker whose grandmother offered the first cigarette when she was a little girl of seven. I could not possibly know what temptations have brought them to the struggles they face today. Furthermore, God is not particularly impressed with my abstinence when it has cost me nothing in pain or tears or repeated attempts at cure.

The point of all this is that we don't know what goes on in other people's hearts, and we need to have a great humility in dealing with those who struggle with temptations we know nothing about.

PRINCIPLES FOR DEALING WITH SEXUAL ABUSE

Without question, the most difficult kind of confrontation of all is that which involves sexual abuse. There are several reasons for this:

1. Such a sin, when viewed in the light of day and the distance of time, seems so unspeakable—certainly to the victim and probably to the perpetrator—that those involved can hardly bear any verbalizing of what happened. It seems, somehow, that if the abuse is never actually stated, it will not "feel" quite as bad.

2. Sexual abuse is nearly always committed *because* there is some special relationship of love and trust; as a result, the victim is left with mixed, confused feelings about what has happened and what it meant.

3. Sexual abuse is often driven deep into the unconscious mind of the victim because it is too difficult to handle, and then it resurfaces years later in a difficult marriage relationship or in other damaging responses to life.

4. Because sexual abuse is often against very young children, the victim feels trapped in a situation over which he or she has no control. That helplessness may later turn into anger at other relationships in which the victim has no control.

By the time a victim of sexual abuse is ready for confrontation, the guilty person may be very elderly, ill, or perhaps even deceased. The distance between the time of the event and the confrontation may encourage other family members to advise the victim, "Forget and get on with your life." Still, the issue may require confrontation if there is to be healing and forgiveness.

In *The Wounded Heart: Hope for Adult Victims of Childhood Sexual Abuse*, Dr. Dan Allender writes:

> *In order to love, we must both honor the dignity and expose the depravity of the person with whom we are in relationship. We cannot love if we distance ourselves or overlook the damage of another's sin; neither can we love if we fail to move into another's world to offer a taste of life. In both cases, the lover often is a martyr for the sake of the gospel, sacrificing personal comfort for the sake of helping the other experience his own longings and need for grace.*[3]

It's a tough order—to challenge the awful offense involved when sexual molestation has occurred; and it would certainly take a great measure of the grace of God to "honor the dignity" of that "loved" perpetrator, even in the process of confrontation. But both, says Dr. Allender, are necessary.

"But why *must* such terrible secrets be dragged out into the open?" we are tempted to ask. "If it all happened long ago when the victim was a child, what purpose would be served in reopening the wound and disgracing the perpetrator (family member, close family friend, clergyman, or neighbor)?"

If, indeed, such damaging events from the past could simply be written off without any later consequences, it would seem a logical way to deal with the problem.

But sexual abuse *does* have serious consequence in the life of the one who has been hurt. Even when a girl who has been sexually abused at an early age seems to have been able to function quite normally for a while, the effects of the abuse often create a lack of trust and a sense of worthlessness.

Kristin A. Kunzman indicates that it is essential for the victim to tell the family about the sexual abuse first, as a way of standing up for oneself as a powerful adult; second, to end the secret and silence of the abuse; third, to quit protecting the abuser; fourth, to stop the abuse cycle and help protect other children; fifth, to open relationships with supportive family members.[4]

Because of the social consequences of such confrontation, it is important for the one who has been hurt to have good spiritual counsel (and probably professional counseling), to handle the matter in the right way.

Whether or not the result of confrontation is exactly what one would like or expect, there has to be a point at which the victim can say, "It is over. I forgive you, and in forgiving you I accept myself as a person important to God. I was not responsible for what happened, but I *do* take the responsibility for using my life to honor that One who loved me and cared enough to die for me." Such words may have to be written in a letter, said in a face-to-face discussion, or spoken over the grave of one already dead; but they *do* need to be said.

All confrontation is difficult, and in the area of sexual sin, there is always the possibility that relationships may be permanently broken. In order to take the right steps and make the wise choices, there will have to be a commitment to thinking as Christ would think, and behaving as He would behave.

It ought to be true, especially within the family of God,

that a compassionate pattern of confrontation would build and encourage good relationships rather than destroy them. In the book, *The Seven Habits of Highly Effective People*, author Stephen R. Covey says:

> *Confrontation takes considerable courage, and many people would prefer to take the course of least resistance, belittling and criticizing, betraying confidences, or participating in gossip about others behind their backs. But in the long run, people will trust and respect you if you are honest and open with them. You care enough to confront. And to be trusted, it is said, is greater than to be loved. In the long run, I am convinced, to be trusted will be also to be loved.*[5]

Perhaps our failure to confront, and to do it biblically, is related to the fact that we do not have enough confidence in the Holy Spirit to go beyond our own words and skills in restoring the one who has hurt us. God does not give us any task to do, however difficult, for which He does not provide His own measure of grace and strength and wisdom. If we value people and value God, then we will do whatever it takes to keep both relationships right.

FIVE

BUILDING PATTERNS OF FORGIVENESS

A group of women waited in the foyer of the church for a bus driver to take them on a special outing. While they chatted, the janitor of the church, a man who had sustained severe injuries in World War II happened to walk by at the end of the hall where the ladies were standing.

One of the women, a visitor to the group, said, "What a strange-looking man. He walks like an ape!" What she did not know was that the wife of that man was in the group. Out of the frozen silence that followed, the wife spoke in a soft voice, "Oh, I'm sorry you don't know my husband; you would realize what a tremendous person he is. He may look rough to you, but to me he is a diamond!"

Few of us, I suspect, would respond with such grace. We have all had times when we wanted to retaliate, to hurl cutting remarks when we or someone dear to us has been hurt by a thoughtless comment, or perhaps by a crushing insult intended to wound. Rarely are we able to contain our anger until it can be vented in a way that will not hurt other people.

In a lifetime of living in the intimate relationships of family, workplace, church and community, we are bound to be offended by the people we rub shoulders with day after day. Unless we build specific patterns for dealing with the offenses, we will be caught off guard and further damage important relationships by our own poor responses.

What is involved in developing good patterns of forgiveness? Patterns are formed by practice. We can choose to work at developing healthy responses. We can establish a daily goal of reflecting a good perspective of ourselves and others. More important—and this is a lifetime process—we can make a determined effort to keep modifying our view of others so that it will line up with God's perspective. *We need to learn to ask the right questions.*

ASK: "WHAT HAPPENED HERE?"

When someone else's actions or words have left you trembling with anger, tell yourself in the simplest terms possible what actually occurred—not what it *felt* like. "The facts, ma'am! Just the facts!"

Once you have established, as fairly as you can, exactly what took place, you need to consider whether or not the "offense" was a planned attempt to hurt you or simply came out of a momentary lapse of control on the part of the offender. Determine not to give more weight to the words spoken than was intended.

At a high school football game, one of the teams was penalized for the unsportsmanlike behavior of a particular boy on the team. In a sudden fit of rage, the mother of that boy pulled a gun out of her purse and began firing at random into the crowd of spectators, wounding two people before she was subdued. No reason was immediately clear as to why she had a gun in her purse, but she certainly could not have known ahead of time what would happen. Because she had no patterns of behavior to rely on that would have provided self-control, a moment of anger exploded into terrible violence!

If we lose our ability to keep the ordinary frustrations and disappointments of life in perspective, our responses to upsetting events will become irrational and perhaps even dangerous.

But when we have thought through the situation, what if we have reason to believe the offender deliberately and maliciously wanted to cause us grief? Even then, we have to learn to mentally put our anger "on the shelf" until we can work through our own response, and deal with the offense in a way that would bring honor to God.

What are the factors that might have to be considered "extenuating" circumstances, in our appraisal of other people's behavior?

1. Wounded people wound others. One of the perversities of the human heart is that when we are suffering, it is easy to become absorbed in our own pain. It is also true that when we hurt, we often want other people to hurt too! We resent their pleasure when we feel so unhappy. And, against all logic, a person who has been hurt often blames the people around him and, consciously or unconsciously, attempts to "get even" by inflicting pain on the very ones who care the most.

If we could see the people in the light of their past hurts, and understand the source of their scars, I suspect it would not be so difficult to allow room for the responses that so often aggravate us. Unfortunately, that isn't a gift most of us acquire easily. Norman Wright says:

> I find that many individuals have difficulty letting loose of their resentments. Not too many people are born with the capacity of forgiving. It is a response that must be learned. The believer has the greater opportunity to learn and practice this because of being a forgiven person.[1]

2. Men and women operate differently in relationships. Sharon, frustrated that her husband sometimes forgot her birthdays and often made fun of her need for romantic or emotional responses in their relationship, discussed the

problems of her marriage with an older friend.

Her friend suggested several steps she might take to encourage a more expressive and romantic relationship, but then concluded by saying, "The bottom line is that you will have to remember men always think like men, and women think like women."

Sharon's eyes snapped in frustration. "That's what everybody keeps saying, but that's what makes me so angry; men are just so . . . so . . . male!"

And they are. By the same token, women are just so . . . so . . . female! When we are struggling to understand some aspect of the opposite gender (or our own, for that matter!) we must register into our emotional computer an acceptance of those unique differences as they were designed by God, and consciously "forgive" whatever gender qualities may irritate or confuse!

3. Personalities do not always mesh. Although a later chapter discusses this problem more fully, let me give an illustration here. Susan is a perfectionist. She has a strong penchant for justice, holds high expectations for herself and others, and feels a great deal of impatience with others who do not do things her way. God has been using the circumstances of her life to modify and refine this mentality, but it is a problem that she has to face on a daily basis. It often comes up in her prayers.

On the other hand, Carl, her husband, is laid back, witty, a little messy, and often late. Although Susan has sometimes asked the Lord for help in developing a more relaxed approach to living, for the capacity to get less hung up on nonessentials, for the ability to be less time-conscious and pressured, she confesses that she often still struggles. She becomes irritable when Carl arrives thirty minutes late for a meal and often plays the role of disapproving parent with him. "If there were two people living in this house with personalities like Carl's, the health department would close down the place!" she says ruefully. "But if both of us were like me, we would both be in a psychiatric hospital!" Fortunately, when God puts together two people who seem not to "fit," He gives the oil of His grace to make it possible for the friction to be reduced.

4. We all see life from a limited viewpoint. Sidney Harris says, "Society is like a pot of soup; it needs different and contrasting ingredients to give it body and flavor."

If only we really believed that! How much more fun life would be if we could enjoy our own uniqueness and that of others.

We are all products of our culture, our upbringing, our education, our gender, and the genetic ingredients we have inherited from generations of our forebears. Even in a single family there are enough differences in the ways various members look at life to create conflicts that require daily forgiveness. If we insist on unilateral agreement about everything, total understanding, and absolute perfection in the personalities of those closest to us, we deny and invalidate the very characteristics designed by God for both our happiness and our growth. This is especially true in marriage. Someone has said that our mate's flaws are intended by God to be the sandpaper that smooths down our own imperfections. But marriage is not the only source of spiritual sandpaper! Any relationship that is significant—because of common job responsibilities, family connections, or church involvement—may be used of God to make us more like Himself.

Not long ago, when I was going through old journals, tracing the ways God had used people to work on my own imperfections, I found these lines I had written at a difficult time. Perhaps you will identify with them:

> Lord, is this the tool
>   that You have brought into my life
>   to fashion gentleness?
> I, who have rushed through life
>   slam-banging my way
>   with flashing eyes

and ready answers—
Eager to fix the world?

I, who loved truth
  saw truth only in the codes,
  the rituals and the rules.
What I failed to see is that mercy
  knows more of truth than law—
The grace of God sees life more clearly
  than any ancient sacrifice.

The neat constructions of my values,
  my well-designed beliefs—
My expectations of Yourself and others
  lie broken in the wreckage of lost dreams.

So what do I have left on which to lean?
  Well, the Word is still there,
Clean and undistorted by my foolish presuppositions.
  Those I loved and wanted to change—
They are there too, waiting and expectant
  for the work that You will do in me.

And You are there—have been—will be—
  forever the same,
Watching in Your patience for the ashes to settle
  till I am free, humbled and cleansed—
A living example of the grace of God. (1985)

ASK: "WAS MY RESPONSE APPROPRIATE?"

1. Did I reveal hidden anger? Have I used this incident or circumstance to vent bitterness left over from some other experience?

Angela and Paula were next-door neighbors and good friends. Angela's daughter often baby-sat for Paula's little boy, and they frequently shared recipes and books.

One day when Paula turned into her driveway, Angela called out a greeting from the flower bed she was weeding, "Hi! How's it going?"

Paula answered with an abrupt, "Fine," and turned to go into the house without another word. Angela was stunned; obviously something was wrong but she hadn't the slightest idea what it could be. After making several more unsuccessful attempts to renew what had been a good relationship, Angela asked her children if they knew what could be wrong. Petie, her youngest son, was able to give her a clue.

"Well, she fussed at me the other day because she said we let our dog do his business in her yard."

"But that isn't possible," Angela said. "You know we always keep the dog's leash fastened to the clothesline."

"Yeah, I know, but it's long enough for the dog to get under her bushes."

Angela immediately shortened the dog's leash and then went next door to apologize to her neighbor.

"I am so sorry, Paula. I had no idea the dog was messing up your yard. I've fixed the problem. Will you forgive me?"

Paula dropped her head in embarrassment. "Oh, Angela! I *did* make a big deal out of the problem with the dog, but I really don't think that's what I'm mad about. We found out last week that my husband is going to have to stay in the Navy two more years, and I was counting on going home to Virginia this year. I'm *really* angry with the Navy!"

How often our surface reactions come out of some bitterness or frustration that we may not even have recognized or acknowledged!

2. Do I have unrealistic expectations? Am I insisting on the fulfillment of youthful ideals, the romantic dream? James Johnson writes:

> *Christianity is too often sold as the invitation to a Disneyland fantasy world. "Security, safety, and enjoyment" is too often the slogan that beguiles, and*

this sets up God as a kindly grandfather ready to unload all the glories, wonders, and treasures of life that could not be attained prior to conversion. The blow of unrealized expectation in critical areas leaves the Christian wallowing in self-pity perhaps more than those not Christian. It is a case of saying, "God does not really love me, or He wouldn't put me through this!"[2]

Perhaps more than any generation, we have grown up to believe that being a "nice person," loving God, and doing all the "right" things will keep us from having to face the disappointment of financial failure, broken health, damaged relationships, or unfulfilled dreams. Like Job, struggling with unbelievable disappointment and heartache, we must ask ourselves, "Shall we accept good from God, and not trouble?" (Job 2:10)

In his book, *How to Disciple Your Children*, Walter Henrichsen writes:

Life is impossible to understand apart from a personal relationship with Jesus Christ. Even as Christians there is much we cannot understand. We spoil our children when we communicate to them that life is a bowl of cherries, nothing bad happens to Christians, or that our children should be able to understand all that comes into their lives. Their confidence must never be in us. It must never be in their ability to understand. It must only be in the character of God and His unfailing commitment to them.[3]

Kitty was a gifted chemist and enjoyed her work developing new products for a major industrial chemical company. The one drawback to her pleasure was a boss who resented sometimes being overshadowed by the successful projects of a lesser employee who happened to be a woman! After months of working on a particularly significant product which would save the company thousands of dollars, Kitty prepared her report for the company officials. Imagine her surprise afterward when she discovered her efforts had been presented to the company officials as the work of her boss!

As it turned out, the president of the company had done a little research of his own and identified Kitty as the rightful recipient of the company bonus. Her boss, however, was never publicly reprimanded, and he was retained as head of the department.

Kitty's initial response was one of anger; but she liked her job, and she understood that she would always have to deal with the extreme competitiveness of her field, in this company or in some other. She chose to keep on doing her work enthusiastically and carefully, allowing God to determine how He would handle the problem of "fairness."

ASK: "HAVE I ACKNOWLEDGED MY CULPABILITY IN THIS RELATIONSHIP?"

When a relationship has been damaged, it is always easier to see with clarity the guilt of the person who has hurt us than to see our own guilt.

When my own children were small, I often found it difficult to discern where to place the blame when a quarrel erupted. Just as I was getting ready to punish one child for hitting or kicking another, I often discovered that the supposed "victim" had been teasing or deliberately provoking the one I was about to punish!

Unfortunately, we do not easily outgrow this inability to recognize and accept our part in any misunderstanding; nor do we admit to our own responsibility for controlling our responses to what we cannot change. We go through life looking at ourselves and our own motives through protective colored glass, while we view others under the glaring spotlight of our own requirements for the ideal, the unreachable.

TAKE RESPONSIBILTY FOR YOUR OWN LIFE AND CHOICES

Learn to quit blaming others for what has happened and carefully plan ways of turning the pain of lost dreams and unfulfilled longings into something that will produce blessing to others and thus glorify God. Philippians 2:12-13 says, "Continue to work out your salvation with fear and trembling, for it is God who works in you to will and to act according to His good purpose." Working out one's own salvation does not mean earning it. It simply means that the power of God—to behave humbly and responsibly—is activated in the person who chooses to do God's will.

1. Your forgiving someone will be speeded up if you seek forgiveness from anyone *you* have wronged. You may have to make restitution as you discover the extent of your own wrongdoing, but you will quickly discover how much easier it is to forgive others once you have faced and acknowledged your own failures. Ultimately, what makes forgiving others a more manageable pill to swallow is a daily practice of seeking forgiveness from the Lord Himself. "If we confess our sins, He is faithful and just and will forgive us our sins and purify us from all unrighteousness" (1 John 1:9).

2. Work daily at learning to forget the past—past personal failure, past hurt by others, past disappointment. Sometimes it is good to ask the Lord to give you the blessing of a bad memory when it comes to things that need to be forgotten. Like the Apostle Paul, you then can say:

> *Not that I have already obtained all this, or have already been made perfect, but I press on to take hold of that for which Christ Jesus took hold of me. Brothers, I do not consider myself yet to have taken hold of it. But one thing I do: Forgetting what is behind and straining toward what is ahead, I press on toward the goal to win the prize for which God has called me heavenward in Christ Jesus (Philippians 3:12-14).*

3. Learn to walk day by day with humility and faith. First Peter 5:6 tells us, "Humble yourselves, therefore, under God's mighty hand, that He may lift you up in due time." PATIENCE!

4. Be willing to work consistently on your own life, building new habits, new responses, and where required, developing a new lifestyle. Expect your growth to be ongoing. "Commit your way to the Lord; trust in Him and He will do this: He will make your righteousness shine like the dawn, the justice of your cause like the noonday sun" (Psalm 37:5-6).

5. Learn from your mistakes. Develop a good understanding of cause and effect. Start observing consequences. Accept the biblical warning, "A man reaps what he sows" (Galatians 6:7), and seek the Lord's help in making your good responses the seed that will grow into healthy relationships.

6. Rest in the sovereign wisdom and mercy of God that reconstructs the broken pieces of your life to make something more precious than you could have experienced apart from His grace. Ask, "How does God fit into the picture of what has happened?" Remember:

He knows what has happened.

He allowed what happened to happen.

He loves you and cares about you beyond what you could imagine.

He understands how you feel.

His will for you is not derailed by what happened.

He accepted you just the way you were, loved you when you were unlovable, forgave the unforgivable, covered with His own blood your sins and failures so that He could have fellowship with you.

Everything He has done for you He has also done, wants to do, or is doing for that person who has wounded you so deeply.

He requires that your ultimate relationship with anyone who has hurt you be like His relationship with you.

He gives the grace to help you do what may seem impossible. He says of Himself, "With God all things are possible" (Matthew 19:26).

7. Become a serious student of the Word of God. Expect and search for answers to the great questions of your life.

> *Do not let this Book of the Law depart from your mouth; meditate on it day and night, so that you may be careful to do everything written in it. Then you will be prosperous and successful. Have I not commanded you? Be strong and courageous. Do not be terrified; do not be discouraged, for the Lord your God will be with you wherever you go (Joshua 1:8-9).*

"Grace is the face God wears when He meets our imperfections, sin, weakness, and failure," David Seamands says. "Grace is what God is and what God does when He meets the sinful and undeserving. Grace is pure gift, free for the taking."[4]

When we understand what God's grace has made possible for us, then we will know how to make grace work in our hearts to build patterns of forgiveness toward others.

SIX

BEING "HUMAN" AND BEING "EVIL"

n the fall of 1993, when the American Fertility Society announced an experiment in which a human embryo was cloned, the public response was one of horror. *TIME* magazine reported:

> *Once it was out, the news that human embryos had been cloned flew around the world with the speed of sound bites bouncing off satellites. That afternoon the switchboard at George Washington (the university where the experiments took place) logged 250 calls from the press. . . . A spokesman for the Japan Medical Association found the experiment "unthinkable." French President Francois Mitterrand pronounced himself "horrified." The Vatican's L'Osservatore Romano warned in a front-page editorial that such procedures could lead humanity down "a tunnel of madness."[1]*

George Annas, a medical ethicist from Boston University quoted in the *Time* article, argues that it will be only a matter of time "before some entrepreneur tries to market embryos derived from Michael Jordan or Cindy Crawford."[2]

THE GOODNESS OF INDIVIDUALITY

Even aside from the ethical questions related to cloning, most of us would argue that diversity is a good thing and that all of us have a right to our individual identity. As much as we might want other people to think like we do, and as often as we tend to wish that more of us had similarities of viewpoint or taste, we know that individuality is a blessing, not a curse.

However, knowing that diversity in human personality and physique and taste is good does not keep us from *feeling* the frustrations that come with differences.

We are all involved daily in communication clashes, whether hidden or public, with people pursuing goals and schedules different from ours, relating in alien ways, or reacting and responding in words that irritate and confuse.

All too often we accumulate mental and emotional data about other people under headings that imply moral deficiency or personality flaws when, in fact, these bits of information ought to be categorized in terms of uniqueness, individuality, and personhood.

While the word "individuality" is never used in Psalm 139, the unique and personal descriptions in this prayer of David's make it clear that every human personality designed by God is an absolute original. Notice the specific attention God gives to every detail of each individual He creates:

> Patterns of schedule and lifestyle:
> *"You know when I sit and when I rise. . . . You discern my going out and my lying down"* (vv. 2-3).
> Habits and thought patterns:
> *"You perceive my thoughts from afar. . . . You are familiar with all my ways"* (vv. 2-3).

Manner of speech:
> "*Before a word is on my tongue You know it completely*" (v. 4).

Genetic code:
> "*My frame was not hidden from You when I was made in the secret place. When I was woven together in the depths of the earth, Your eyes saw my unformed body*" (vv. 15-16).

Lifespan:
> "*All the days ordained for me were written in Your book before one of them came to be*" (v. 16).

Conscience:
> "*Search me, O God, and know my heart; test me and know my thoughts. See if there is any offensive way in me*" (vv. 23-24).

The psalmist's glorious conclusion to all this is that for each of us, the sum total of what God put together that makes us uniquely ourselves is by special design and it is good. "For You created my inmost being; You knit me together in my mother's womb. I praise You because I am fearfully and wonderfully made; Your works are wonderful, I know that full well" (vv. 13-14).

Can it be that I have refused to accept in another person those special qualities designed by God? How much pleasure I will miss if I fail to appreciate the unlimited diversity of God's creation that made us, even with our common roots, so totally our own selves!

As far as I know, no one has ever made a list of the fifty most common idiosyncrasies that drive other people crazy, but most of us could compile a collection of the mannerisms and responses we see in those closest to us!

I have a brother-in-law, Roger, a seminary professor who is one of the smartest people I know. He can give you a rundown of church history, complete with dates, at the snap of a finger. To entertain himself when he has to wait on other people, he mentally lists all the Chicago Cubs teams since 1946, or the catchers in the National League for 1993.

Despite all his gifts of memory, he qualifies for the title of Absentminded Professor. Actually I base his title on one incident.

One night his wife, Joy, woke with a pounding headache. When Roger sensed there was a problem, he asked, "What can I do to help?"

"Could you bring me a couple of aspirin?" Joy asked.

Roger climbed out of bed and headed for the bathroom. After a long delay, he returned to the bedroom, crawled into bed and turned over on his side.

"What about my aspirin?" Joy asked.

Roger sat up in bed with a start. "Good grief!" he said. "I took them!"

In his book, *Love and Marriage*, Bill Cosby describes a bedtime ritual in his home, in which his wife, without fail, questions whether or not he has remembered to lock the front door. He always replies that he has taken care of it.

> At this point in our little performance in the theatre of the absurd, she will not say, "I don't believe you"; but a few minutes later, she will go downstairs and check all the locks. It is nothing personal; it is simply that women do not trust people of a foreign sex.[3]

CAUSES OF FRUSTRATION

All of us could tell stories describing the funny, weird or frustrating characteristics of the people we are closest to, but it would be impossible for anyone to construct a comprehensive tabulation of all the traits that bug other human beings; what drives me up the wall may seem charming and endearing to someone else.

Still, there are a few typically rocky places where the red flags are most apt to go up:

1. Bad family patterns. People who have grown up in homes where there has been alcoholism, abuse, divorce, neglect, or extreme poverty, often bring the damage of these hurts into other relationships. This offers a special challenge to those married to partners from such a background, to apply the soothing ointment of grace and patience to every blister that rises to the surface in the daily contacts of living together.

2. Ethnic diversities. While we don't appreciate stereotypes, it is true that our particular ethnic background may influence the way we relate to other people. Cultures handle conflicts differently. Some encourage family discussion of problems, perhaps with voices raised. It is all part of the family style. Other groups or nationalities consider any kind of discussion of problems to be bad manners.

The view of marriage itself, and particularly a view of roles in marriage, varies widely in different cultures, and this can create conflict for partners reared with divergent standards and taboos.

The observance of traditions and holidays which run counter to what a newcomer in the group has experienced can create major difficulties in relationships.

When my husband and I were first married, I looked forward to being a part of the large Swedish Christmas celebration traditional in his family. I was eager to contribute my own culinary specialties at the Christmas smorgasbord. I knew there would be roast pork, lutefisk served with mustard gravy, rice pudding, fruit soup, pickled herring and smoked salmon, and I had heard about the homemade root beer made with yeast which had to be drunk before the bottles exploded! I pictured how some of my own family recipes might become absorbed into the tradition. I was even willing to tackle some of the traditional Swedish dishes, if given the chance to practice. But when the assignments were given out, I was asked to bring the relish tray! They were trying to take the pressure off a new bride; *I* assumed they didn't trust my cooking abilities!

3. Personality characteristics. In his book, *Why You Act the Way You Do*, Tim LaHaye analyzes the four primary temperaments: sanguine, choleric, melancholic and phlegmatic. Because individuals rarely fit entirely within one group, he then describes the most common blends of temperament. For the sake of illustration, imagine that this melancholic woman is married to the sanguine man.

> *Melancholy housewives and mothers are easily the best housekeepers and cooks. Dinner is always on time. But they might lack gracious flexibility. Woe to the child who tracks mud all over the freshly scrubbed kitchen floor! Or woe to the salesman husband who gets home late for dinner because he had to finalize that "big sale" at quitting time![4]*
>
> *Sanguines rarely get ulcers; we have already seen that they usually give them to everyone else. Since people are a major cause of pressure and sanguines love to be around people, they are never far from pressure, which usually they helped to create.*
>
> *These lighthearted people are often very disorganized, generally arrive late for meetings, and are rarely prepared for whatever they are supposed to do.[5]*

Since we are often inclined to marry those with characteristics opposite our own, the conflicts between differing personalities in one family are probably more "normal" than we expect them to be.

4. Birth order. Our position in the family has a lot to do with the way we relate to other people. For instance, Kevin Leman describes firstborn people as generally being "organized, overparented, overprotected, pressured to perform, achievers, conservative, and wanting control."[6]

These characteristics, says Leman, may be expressed differently, since firstborns can be either compliant and wanting to please, or strong-willed and aggressive.

Middle children are most directly influenced by the sibling just above in age and often feel crowded out in the growing up process, getting neither the pressure to succeed which the oldest child gets nor the special attention of the baby in the family. "Middle-born children," says Leman, "are very susceptible to believing they only count when they avoid conflict because they've been negotiating and mediating all through life."

On the other hand, "Youngest children in the family are typically the outgoing charmers, the personable manipulators. They are also affectionate, uncomplicated, and sometimes a little absentminded. Their 'space cadet' approach to life gets them laughs, smiles, and shakes of the head."[7]

It isn't hard to figure out the complications that come when various mixes of these qualities meet in marriage or working relationships.

No attempt is made here to provide a total picture of any specific position in the family. My point in mentioning any general characteristic is simply to illustrate the fact that whatever our place in the family, it will affect the way we interact with other people and it will also influence the way other people perceive us.

5. Gender. While it is clear that there are rather obvious differences in the ways men and women respond to circumstances and to people, scientists have never been able to prove conclusively which patterns are biologically induced and which are learned responses. Perhaps influenced by the femininist movement, sociologists taught that men gravitated toward professions that involved great concentrations of math skills and logic simply because they were conditioned to do so. Women, on the other hand, were encouraged by society to value marriage and motherhood, because it was the traditionally accepted female role.

Recent gender studies have indicated more dramatic biological differences between men and women than were formerly recognized.

> In medicine, researchers documented that heart disease strikes men at a younger age than it does women and that women have a more moderate physiological response to stress. Researchers found subtle neurological differences between the sexes both in the brain's structure and in its functioning. In addition, another generation of parents discovered that, despite their best efforts to give baseballs to their daughters and sewing kits to their sons, girls still flocked to dollhouses while boys clambered into tree forts. Perhaps nature is more important than nurture after all.[8]

We may never satisfactorily solve the problem of why men and women behave differently. A more pertinent problem for us may be learning how to react to gender qualities in those we love, when they just don't seem to make sense to us!

A group of approximately fifty people gathered at our house not long ago for a Sunday School class social. One group of men was in the den watching the last quarter of a football game. They emerged only to refill coffee cups or Coke glasses. In the kitchen a group of women discussed recipes, cold remedies, and the advantages/disadvantages of home schooling. A mixed group in the living room entertained each other trading off "Women always . . ." and "Men always . . ." epithets:

"Men always go for food that has zero nutrition!"

"Women always answer logic with tears!"

"Men think they are communicating when they say, 'Uh huh!' "

"A woman thinks a socket wrench is a sprained elbow!"

In a party setting, where men and women can comfortably interact, the distinctions between male and female responses can be treated as a joke. But in the day-by-day responses of living and working together, more is required. We must continually remind ourselves who is the Author of the plan that makes us male or female.

6. The irritabilities of pain or pressure. Years ago, when I was acting department head at a Christian college, I served on a committee with other department heads, planning curriculum and designing academic programs. I enjoyed the interchange with colleagues I respected and enjoyed.

One man on the committee, however, kept me in a constant state of frustration! Whatever ideas others presented he often shot down; creativity expressed by others on the committee was often drowned in his own negative responses. Everyone soon learned they had to work around the attitudes of one depressing person!

After these meetings I often complained to my husband that this man was "impossible" to work with.

One Saturday morning on a cold winter day something happened that forever changed my perception of this "impossible" committee member.

Our son Jim was working his way through college as a mechanic for church buses, and he occasionally worked on the cars of the college professors as well. This particular man had asked if Jim had time on Saturday to do some work on his car.

And so, while our son worked on the car in our garage, my husband and I spent the entire Saturday morning drinking tea and talking in our home with my "difficult" coworker. In our long conversation, I discovered a fact I had never known; this man (who has long since gone to heaven) had a chronic illness that kept him in constant pain. He fulfilled major responsibilities in life even while enduring a great deal of physical suffering. When he left our house that day, I wanted to put my arms around him and say, "Well, bless your heart! No wonder you've been such a grouch!" Of course I didn't, but I never again saw that man without praying that God would give him grace, and I never again reacted with frustration to what I felt he was unable to change.

I was reminded of a quotation Miss Edith Torrey gave us in a college Bible class. I have never seen it in print, but Miss Torrey attributed it to her father, Dr. R.A. Torrey: "What appears to you to be flaws in another's character may, instead, be the scars from some well-fought battle."

Living in a world full of human beings is indeed like trying to "dance with porcupines." We all need to work at producing in our lives those qualities that will make it possible for us to live and work together in harmony. It is only through the power of the Holy Spirit that we will be able to make our responses reflect His presence in our lives.

But the fruit of the Spirit is love, joy, peace, patience, kindness, goodness, faithfulness, gentleness and self-control. Against such things there is no law. Those who belong to Christ Jesus have crucified the sinful nature with its passions and desires. Since we live by the Spirit, let us keep in step with the Spirit. Let us not become conceited, provoking and envying each other (Galatians 5:22-26).

SEVEN

THE GOAL OF DISCIPLINE AND FORGIVENESS: RESTORATION

The headlines are full of depressing reminders that something is drastically wrong with our society:

MOVIE IDOL DIES OF AIDS
FAMILY SPY RING UNCOVERED
MAYOR INDICTED FOR BRIBERY
SIXTEEN-YEAR-OLD SLAYS FATHER
ATHLETE DIES FROM DRUG OVERDOSE
CORPORATION INVOLVED IN NATIONWIDE FRAUD

When we read such news, we are tempted to grab our children and try to escape to some quiet, safe place where our families will not be contaminated by a world sick with sin.

It is especially frightening to discover that "the world" makes inroads into our families, even when we are working very hard to establish a home based on the Word of God. Our four-year-old shocks us with gutter language he has picked up we know not where! Our Christian teenagers crave the lifestyle of rock stars. Our own spiritual goals are often submerged in a materialism we hardly know we possess.

What is to be done?

Through the centuries various groups have attempted to withdraw from the culture, setting up colonies in which they could maintain a purity and separation from the world's standards. It is even possible that the Jim Jones cults of the world actually began with some notion that isolation would provide protection from an evil world. They created instead a hothouse where evil, unseen and unchallenged by any outside critic, could explode into destruction and death.

Escape from civilization is hardly the answer! There is no practical way a community of Christians can completely isolate itself from the wicked influence of the world around it. We are bound by necessity and by obligation to the human race and human civilization on every hand.

As we live in a damaged world, we are going to have to find ways to combat the forces of evil that constantly surround us. Is it possible that God not only wants us to resist the evil things we see in our culture but also to work for changes? Can the body of Christ expect to:

Infiltrate the media?
Stop the growth of materialism and humanism?
Significantly influence modern entertainment?
Develop an education system which is wholly "Christian"?
Be a major influence in politics?
Rebuild a national concern for the sanctity of home and family?
Develop a new respect for honor and integrity?
Evangelize the entire world?

No. Unfortunately, we will not usher in the millenium by wonderful changes in government, in the arts, in science, in education or in psychology. We will not even convert the world to a state of righteousness by our preaching and teaching and godly living. The prophecy given by Jesus Christ Himself in John 12:31 has not yet taken place,

"Now is the time for judgment on this world; now the prince of this world will be driven out." We are still waiting for that day when "that ancient serpent, who is the devil, or Satan" will be "locked and sealed" for a thousand years (Revelation 20:2).

Still, it is true that we *are* to be both "the salt of the earth" and "the light of the world" (see Matthew 5:13-16), and it is impossible for salt and light *not* to have influence upon the environment. We ought to both expose and enlighten; through the Holy Spirit within us, we should expect to make a difference in helping to cure and heal the effects of sin.

That statement also defines our relationship to one who has done wrong, whether in the church or outside of it. Church discipline for a member who has seriously erred, or discipline of children who have done wrong in the home, has three goals:

1. To expose and identify sin; to teach the sinner that what he has done is wrong.

2. To create a climate (or attitude) that will encourage change; to help the sinner come to repentance and ultimately to seek conformity to the image of Christ.

3. To restore relationships within the family.

If the process of discipline deals only with identifying sin and punishing the sinner, then the discipline has been a failure.

A SCANDALOUS CASE

One of the most startling cases of church discipline discussed in the Scripture is found in 1 Corinthians 5:9-13. The Apostle Paul wrote to the Christians at Corinth:

> *I have written you in my letter not to associate with sexually immoral people—not at all meaning the people of this world who are immoral, or the greedy and swindlers, or idolaters. In that case you would have*

*to leave this world. But now I am writing you that
you must not associate with anyone who calls himself a brother but is sexually immoral or greedy, an
idolater or a slanderer, a drunkard or a swindler.
With such a man do not even eat. . . . Expel the wicked man from among you.*

The sinner in this case was having an affair with his own
mother-in-law! Apparently he was so popular in the
church that no one was confronting his wrongdoing.

Paul's letter shocked the church into action. Their obedience to the apostle's commands was evidently immediate and thorough. They fulfilled steps one and two of the
discipline process but failed to understand that the final
goal of discipline was restoration. When Paul wrote a second letter, he told the church what was yet lacking:

*I wrote you out of great distress and anguish of heart
and with many tears, not to grieve you but to let you
know the depth of my love for you. If anyone has
caused grief, he has not so much grieved me as he
has grieved all of you, to some extent—not to put it
too severely. The punishment inflicted on him by the
majority is sufficient for him. Now instead, you ought
to forgive and comfort him, so that he will not be
overwhelmed by excessive sorrow. I urge you, therefore, to reaffirm your love for him. The reason I wrote
you was to see if you would stand the test and be
obedient in everything. If you forgive anyone, I also
forgive him. And what I have forgiven—if there was
anything to forgive—I have forgiven in the sight of
Christ for your sake, in order that Satan might not
outwit us. For we are not unaware of his schemes
(2 Corinthians 2:4-11).*

Notice the way in which discipline is to be carried out in
the church:

1. The challenger of evil must not be one who speaks out of pride or vengeance, not a "finger-pointer." He must be one whose own heart is saddened and grieved. Paul said he wrote "out of great distress and anguish of heart . . . to let you know the depth of my love for you." *We cannot restore if we do not love!*

2. Discipline is a reminder of the far-reaching effects of sin. When one person sins, many people are hurt. "He has not so much grieved me as he has grieved all of you."

3. Forgiveness and restoration are far more than a cold dismissal of the charge; they are inextricably involved in comforting the one who has sinned and seeks forgiveness; "Comfort him, so that he will not be overwhelmed by excessive sorrow."

Perhaps more than anything else, the person who has sinned needs those who are important to him to "reaffirm" their love for him, just as Paul commanded the Corinthian church to do. Instead, we often grudgingly acknowledge that the sinner has been forgiven, but we suggest by our attitude that he is forever somehow "tainted" and therefore never again completely accepted in the "inner circle" of our fellowship. We want to make it clear that we have done our duty, but we subtly convey that this person is something of an embarrassment, a blot on our reputation! In responding as we do, we miss the opportunity to show to our children and to every other struggling human being that we have a "God of the second chance."

I do not believe it is the incidence of failure in the life of a Christian that brings disgrace on the cause of Christ so much as it is the way we respond—the sinner to his own sin and the saint to the sinner!

There *are* exceptions. One of the most heartwarming stories I ever heard of corporate forgiveness and restoration involved a pastor of a large church who fell into sin. Once his confession and repentance were expressed, and the shock and disappointment of the congregation were dealt with, the church arranged for their pastor, now out of the pulpit, to have two full years of counseling and spiritual restoration—all at their own expense. Imagine how their love and kindness worked in the life of that heartbroken man! After the two years, the church planned a major banquet to honor his restoration. Like the father of the prodigal son, they gave him a gold ring to mark the occasion and a new suit of clothes. They celebrated with tears and rejoicing the fact that Satan's work had been thwarted. God had brought glory to Himself through the response of those who had learned to confront, to restore, and to love!

4. Forgiveness on the part of one who has been hurt opens the door to forgiveness on the part of others who may have also been hurt. As Paul said, "If you forgive anyone, I also forgive him. And what I have forgiven . . . I have forgiven in the sight of Christ for your sake."

Many children go through life hating a father they should have been able to love. Because they never saw forgiveness on the part of a resentful mother, they carried their own unforgiveness through a lifetime!

We need to remember our forgiveness is a visable sign to the world of Christ's forgiveness which is already completed in the heart of one who has acknowledged and forsaken his sin.

5. Here's a point we often miss: We must forgive in order that Satan's work will be brought to a halt. Paul acknowledged that his forgiveness was "in order that Satan might not outwit us. For we are not unaware of his schemes."

Satan likes to tell us, in tempting us to do wrong, "This isn't really such a bad, terrible, horrible sin." Then once we have fallen into temptation, he says, "You know, this thing you have done is really unforgivable. You might as well give up. God could never use you again."

We must be sure that we never allow Satan to win a victory by the way we respond to sin—our own or someone else's.

In his book, *When a Good Man Falls*, Erwin W. Lutzer writes:

> *Unfortunately, there are many believers whose lives have never been mended; there are broken bones in the body of Christ that have never been properly set. Many fruitful Christians hobble out of joint, never able to gain their spiritual equilibrium. Restoration means that a fallen believer is back in full fellowship with God and the church. Although he may not always be restored to his former ministry, he is befriended and received fully as a member of the body of believers.*[1]

WHEN THE SINNER PERSISTS IN EVIL

What if a person does wrong and, in spite of all attempts to restore, he chooses to continue in a path of evil? When this question was brought up by the disciples, Jesus told them:

> *If your brother sins against you, go and show him his fault, just between the two of you. If he listens to you, you have won your brother over. But if he will not listen, take one or two others along, so that "every matter may be established by the testimony of two or three witnesses." If he refuses to listen to them, tell it to the church; and if he refuses to listen even to the church, treat him as you would a pagan or a tax collector (Matthew 18:15-17).*

Without question, these instructions would imply that such a person was no longer a member of the fellowship in good standing and would not be given any place of honor or authority. It could also mean that such a person would be considered untrustworthy, just as a biblical tax collector was considered to be. Paul's instructions to the

Corinthian church regarding an unrepentant believer included, "With such a man do not even eat" (1 Corinthians 5:11). The reference here is to the church fellowship, perhaps specifically to the taking of Communion together. I do not believe it is to be applied to family relationships, but is rather the excluding of an individual who goes on stubbornly in his sin from the special fellowship that signifies a common bond in worshiping the Lord.

I have seen cases of church discipline in which I felt the congregation gave up too soon in trying to restore a fallen believer to righteousness. If we quickly remove all contact with one who has sinned, then who will be the prod toward repentance? Do we not leave the person prey to only ungodly influences?

A young man who was very dear to me, as he was to his own father and mother, chose to forsake all the godly elements of his young life. For seven long years he wandered far away from the Lord, experiencing and tasting every possible pleasure the world had to offer. Even though his parents were heartbroken at the life he was leading, he never called home without their reminding him that they loved him and would never stop loving him. They also reminded him that God would never stop pursuing him and that their prayers would follow wherever he went. When he finally hit bottom, they were the ones who paid off the drug dealers threatening his life; they were the ones who saw him through rehabilitation and restoration; they were the ones who held on until that young man became a shining example of the grace of God! Now he works with other young rebels, serving as chaplain for a large public high school football team and forming Christian support groups for young addicts.

In the years that young man was away from the Lord I often thought, "This looks hopeless." I know I would have been tempted to give up too soon, but his parents did not. Perhaps the secret was that they loved him more than I. Could that be the secret of all restoration?

A WARNING TO US ALL

One final word about restoration. When we are dealing with the sinner, we must never forget that no matter how horrendous his sins may be, his guilt did not begin when he got caught! Evil is not evil simply because the person has been found out.

First Timothy 5:24 says, "The sins of some men are obvious, reaching the place of judgment ahead of them; the sins of others trail behind them" or show up later. When we look at "public" sinners, we need to remember that our own sins will just as surely be brought to light. God sees the secrets of our hearts, and someday they will all be revealed. This ought to instill in us a humility and compassion as we work with those whose sins have been made public; it should warn us of our own vulnerability to sin.

In the problem of forgiveness, we must deal not only with what a person has done but also with who he or she is. And as we examine our own hearts, we must face not only what we have done but what we know ourselves to be. Remember, we are dealing not only with humanness, but with depravity. We are dealing not only with individual sins, but also with a nature that at its deepest level is unspeakably flawed by sin.

The solutions are not to be found in our own earnest attempts to be good or even in our kindness to others who have failed. If we measure our worthiness in terms of anything we can do, we are all hopeless!

But there is an answer: it is through the window of God's grace that we see a clear picture of what to do with the problem of sin.

If God is for us, who can be against us? He who did not spare His own Son, but gave Him up for us all—how will He not also, along with Him, graciously give us all things? Who will bring any charge against

those whom God has chosen? It is God who justifies.
Who is he that condemns? Christ Jesus, who died—
more than that, who was raised to life—is at the right
hand of God and is also interceding for us (Romans
8:31-34).

We are not hopeless captives of our own sinful condition. We have One who knows what we are and who chose to pay the ransom for our sins. Whatever we are, whatever we have done, He pleads with us to leave all the weight of our guilt with Him and to accept the gift of His grace!

EIGHT

IS ANY SIN
UNFORGIVABLE?

'm not sure I can ever forgive my grandfather," Colleen said to me. "He ruined my mother's life; he messed up my life, and now it looks like my daughter has been damaged too!" Colleen was understandably furious. The story she told me was one of incest that had touched three generations, and perhaps four!

"The worst part of it is that I can't do anything about it. I want to blow the whistle on that nasty old man, but my grandmother is dying of cancer, and my mother says this will kill her if it comes out. What can I do?"

NAME OF SIN			
FORGIVABLE?			
FORGIVABLE WITH APOLOGY?			
FORGIVABLE EVENTUALLY?			
UNFORGIVABLE?			

When it comes to the business of forgiveness, most of us wish there were some clear-cut rules that would show us exactly what is required in every situation. In fact, it would remove a lot of personal responsibility for making decisions if there were just some expert to fill in a set of boxes for us like those on the preceding page.

The problem, of course, is that once we started making boxes, we'd have to add a lot more categories like:

FORGIVE AND TRUST AGAIN?	*Yes or No*
FORGIVE AND RESTORE FELLOWSHIP?	*Yes or No*
FORGIVE AFTER CONFRONTATION?	*Yes or No*
FORGIVE BUT REQUIRE COUNSELING?	*Yes or No*

If we were really serious about finding what our responses ought to be when we've been hurt, we might even have to add two more boxes:

ASK FORGIVENESS FOR YOUR OWN CULPABILITY IN THE PROBLEM?	*Yes or No*
ACKNOWLEDGE THIS IS NO BIG DEAL AND FORGET IT?	*Yes or No*

Forgiveness requires a great deal of heart-searching, doesn't it? Beginning with the little things.

Obviously, forgiveness is not something we can take lightly. It requires choices about the way we will respond. Even when we have been hurt over some minor misunderstanding—a misinterpreted comment, a gesture of impatience, a raised voice—we have to choose the responses that will knit and heal rather than wound and isolate those who are close to us.

To ignore a supposed slight and then to sulk is no forgiveness at all. While it would be futile and frustrating to be constantly "turning over the rocks" in every conversation to find out what a speaker means, we should develop patterns of asking appropriate questions when we feel threatened by a comment or action:

"Could you explain that a little more fully?"

"Are you angry with me about something?"

"Has something happened today to bother you?"

"Have I said something that hurt?"

Remember that any questions we ask ought to work toward closeness and understanding; they are not designed to pry or to accuse.

When I first started teaching in a Christian college, I was awed and a little intimidated by the experience and education of many of my colleagues. I wasn't sure I had much to contribute to faculty lounge conversations out of my own wisdom and experience, and so I fell into a pattern that had always worked well with my closest friends—I kidded about my own inexperience and foibles. As I got more comfortable with particular individuals who enjoyed "faculty" jokes, we often teased each other.

One day, after the banter had gotten unusually hilarious, and we had gone back to our offices, a fellow novice teacher appeared at my office door. He had laughed along with others in the faculty lounge, but now his face was serious.

"Why don't you like me?" he asked.

I was puzzled. "But I do like you, Dave. Why would you think I don't?"

"Back in the faculty lounge you were really describing me, weren't you, when you talked about teachers forgetting which class they were supposed to be teaching?"

"Heavens, no, Dave! I didn't know that ever happened to you! I'm the one who went to a Wednesday class when it was only Tuesday! But I thought we were just joking anyway. I'm so sorry I said anything that made you feel bad."

"Well, I've found that people always have messages in the things they kid about, and it hurt my feelings."

I learned a lot that day about both sending and receiving messages; things are not always as they seem to be!

Fortunately, David had the good sense to challenge something that had sounded like a put-down, and I had a chance to explain my own way of dealing with insecurities!

While it is always wise to assume that we are more likely than not to make a big deal out of idle comments that had no special significance to the person who made them, nothing should be left to smolder into bitterness.

WHEN MORE IS REQUIRED

What does God expect of me in rebuilding a damaged relationship? Let's say that the offense is real, not imagined, and perhaps even deliberate. Do I have to maintain a friendship in the process of forgiving someone who has hurt me?

I often heard my mother say, "Nothing matters but people and God!" I'm sure she used that to remind us that *things* are not as valuable as people and God, but the significant point is that people *are* precious, and we appreciate God only as we learn to value people.

Therefore, the goal in every conflict is not just to forgive but to restore fellowship.

1. Go as far as it is in your power to patch up a relationship. Use words and touch, intercession and intermediaries, if necessary, to bring any relationship to its highest, noblest point. Don't ever assume that friendships are disposable, or that other later relationships will "make up" for a friendship that has been broken. There is a sense in which every single individual who has come into

our lives has contributed to who we are. To lightly dismiss the loss of one who has been dear to us is the ultimate in waste and carelessness! People are of supreme value to God and they ought to be to us, as well. The permanent loss of any relationship certainly calls for a certain amount of grieving, even when we have done everything in our power to reestablish it.

2. When there is a broken connection, make it your concern to be courteous and kind.

Don't broadcast your broken relationship to others. Sometimes, whether for conviction or because differences seem irreconcilable, we are no longer able to have close fellowship with someone who has been important in our lives. Do everything in your power to keep the chasm from widening. Determine you will not spread the details to every interested listener.

Don't solicit others to your point of view. When there has been damage between spouses, associates, or friends, we are usually eager to make sure other people understand how we have been hurt; we want people to know who's to blame. You may have to give up your right to "be right," or to explain your side to anyone who will listen. Avoid whispered defenses of your position. Allow God to be your defense.

Don't require your friends to choose sides. One of the sad by-products of the splinterings that have come in the body of Christ is that we not only break fellowship with those who do not agree with our viewpoint, but we also require our friends to break fellowship!

The problem is as old as the church. As the Apostle Paul wrote to the carnal Corinthians:

> *I appeal to you, brothers, in the name of our Lord*
> *Jesus Christ, that all of you agree with one another*
> *so that there may be no divisions among you and*
> *that you may be perfectly united in mind and*
> *thought. My brothers, some from Chloe's household*

> have informed me that there are quarrels among
> you. What I mean is this: One of you says, "I follow
> Paul"; another, "I follow Apollos"; another, "I follow
> Cephas"; still another, "I follow Christ" (1 Corin-
> thians 1:10-12).

We need to ask ourselves the same question Paul asked these young, worldly Christians, "Is Christ divided?"

What is true in the church is true in personal relationships as well. How often lifetime friendships are destroyed because a divorce in one family demands that other families who have been close to the couple now have to choose sides!

After a particularly vicious denominational quarrel that resulted in broken fellowship between several pastors' families, one little girl said to her mother, "I'll be glad when I get to heaven. Then I can love whoever I please!"

3. Be a risk-taker. Allow for the possibility of being taken advantage of. Be the one who actively works at reconciling differences and healing wounds.

If you are working to heal a broken relationship, you may feel that to others you look "like a fool." There is a sense in which you are saying, "I am willing to value you more than you value me," and that is going to look foolish to some! But it is one of the ways we get to be like Christ. In Philippians 2:3-5, we are commanded, "Do nothing out of selfish ambition or vain conceit, but in humility consider others better than yourselves. Each of you should look not only to your own interests, but also to the interests of others. Your attitude should be the same as that of Christ Jesus."

Once we can come to the point of saying to the person who has hurt us, "Whether you value me or not, I will consider you important to me!" we will be responding as Jesus responded.

4. Don't slam the door on future reconciliations. Be careful about responding in the heat of the moment in

such a way that future restoration becomes an impossibility: "I will never speak to you again!" "If you leave, don't ever come back!" "Your children can no longer play with my children."

Take a long look; don't tear down your bridges behind you!

I am always glad for the reminders in the Word of God that even spiritual people have conflicts. One of the most notable examples is the dispute between Barnabas and Paul over Barnabas' nephew, John Mark. This young Christian had followed the famous Paul/Barnabas missionary team for a while, perhaps helping with the luggage, running errands, or writing letters, but after a time he got tired or bored or discouraged and left the team to go home.

Later, when Barnabas suggested he be used again, Paul did not want to give this immature helper another chance. The division between the two senior missionaries became such an issue that each man started his own team; Barnabas was determined not to give up on John Mark.

Somewhere, sometime, reconciliation took place, although the Scripture does not give us the details. All we know is that when Paul was an old man, ill and in prison he instructed Timothy, "Get Mark and bring him with you, because he is helpful to me in my ministry" (2 Timothy 4:11).

The issue for us is not who made the first move to repair the relationship and bring John Mark back into fellowship. The point is that when the conflict occurred, there was not an ugly breach left between Paul and Barnabas that made it impossible for them to ever be friends again.

ALL OR NOTHING AT ALL?

When there has been a break in a relationship, it is a good idea to ask yourself what you would have wanted this friendship to become. Make *that* your goal wherever possible. When conflicts arise in a friendship, don't assume that everything is lost. Sometimes a relationship can become better than it was in the beginning, when the parties involved learn how to handle disagreements and differences compatibly.

5. Don't hand out all-or-nothing ultimatums. If this relationship can never be as close as it once was, then take the next best thing. If not a hug, settle for a handshake!

I once watched a group of junior high girls in a major quarrel over who would be whose best friends. The unspoken rule was that a "best friend" was not allowed to have other friends. Since the most popular girl in the class had refused to play by the rules, she was ostracized by the other girls!

We adults often play that game. We decide that people have to fill some place in our lives which we determine to be essential; if they cannot or will not, we don't want them in our lives at all!

Expect the broken relationship to progress toward healing, not necessarily according to the terms you think someone else has set, but rather in terms of your own ability to respond in a godly way. Make forgiveness a part of your daily interaction with that person.

Act as you would act if he had already said, "I'm sorry."

Act as you would act if everything depended upon you.

Act as you would want God to act toward you, if you had hurt Him ('Nuff sed!)

WHAT ABOUT THOSE IMPOSSIBLE TO FORGIVE?

First, clarify what kinds of injuries your "impossible to forgive" list would include:

Theft of property?

Loss of honor or reputation by gossip?

Murder of someone you love?

Broken promises, broken vows, broken trust, broken home?

Your list will not match someone else's. One wife said, "I can forgive one adulterous act, but not a continued affair." Another wife said, "What made my husband's adultery unforgivable was that he did it in our own home!" A third wife said, "I knew my husband had been unfaithful for years. What I can never forgive is that when he left me, he withdrew from the bank the entire inheritance my folks had left me!"

No matter what you have put on your list of unforgivables, you need to put the list away. Destroy it. Erase it from your mind. Get rid of it as thoroughly as God has destroyed His accusations against you! Whatever you may *think*, whatever you may *feel*, whatever seems *logical* or *fair*, you have to ultimately, finally, learn to forgive those who have hurt you.

However we may prefer to interpret Scripture, we cannot get away from Jesus' plain statement in Matthew 6:14-15: "For if you forgive men when they sin against you, your heavenly Father will also forgive you. But if you do not forgive men their sins, your Father will not forgive your sins."

We must forgive—even the unforgivable. But how is that possible?

1. Keep remembering that whatever you have suffered is something God has allowed, and He wants to glorify Himself through this thing which is so difficult. In her book, *Affliction,* Edith Schaeffer says:

> *Marvel of all marvels—without understanding how it could be—we matter in the battle! We matter to God, moment by moment, day by day, and through the months and years in the hidden places of our thoughts. . . . We need to let God be God . . . experience by experience . . . praying that the Lord won't let us "waste" what is going on in any way: Help me, Lord, to be what You want me to be in this, to learn what You want me to learn . . . to demonstrate what*

You want me to demonstrate, to show in this thing a flashing, vivid reality of the fact that the treasure You have given me is an earthen vessel and that the greatness, the excellency, is all of You, God, and not of me. . . .The satisfying thing is that we are not machines. There is variety, and we are not ten-cent-store pottery. We are handmade from real earth, and the colors are natural, placed there by the Master Potter who knows what He is doing with His beloved "vessels."[1]

2. Keep remembering that God allows disappointment in human resources so that we will learn to depend on Him completely. As long as our human desires are satisfied with other human beings, we will never discover the wonderful truth that "God is enough."

Isobel Kuhn, in her autobiography *In the Arena*, tells about her eagerness to serve the Lord as a missionary to China during the war between China and Japan. During the most fruitful time of her ministry, everything collapsed; her husband's work required him to be away from the family constantly, her little daughter was captured by the Japanese, her home was destroyed, her helpers removed. She said of this time:

It seemed as if my last little candle flame of human love had been extinguished. The Superintendency had taken my husband . . . . War had taken my girlie; marriage had taken my Lisu helper; and now home was no longer home. . . . This seemed to be the last straw that broke the camel's back.

I was simply shattered. "You'll never have anyone to love you," mocked Satan, taking advantage of my self-pity. "God is a jealous God. He doesn't want you to have anyone but Him to love you." God was loosening my hold on human love; He was nailing my affections to the cross. . . . The human props on which I leaned so heavily were bound to give way sometime or another, just because they were human. And then when they gave way—how painfully I sprawled! . . . I had surrendered husband, child, friends, all I possessed long ago. But this was something deeper. This was relinquishing my right to them.[2]

3. Keep remembering that trouble is the catalyst for blessing. Life is always a mixture of what is pleasant and what is difficult; it is the difficult things that create spiritual maturity and character, when they are transformed by our choice to accept them cheerfully. And the overflow of our praise affects the lives of others as well.

As servants of God we commend ourselves in every way: in great endurance; in troubles, hardships and distresses . . . through glory and dishonor, bad report and good report; genuine, yet regarded as imposters; known, yet regarded as unknown; dying, and yet we live on; beaten, and yet not killed; sorrowful, yet always rejoicing; poor, yet making many rich; having nothing, and yet possessing everything (2 Corinthians 6:4-10).

Finally, assume that your forgiveness may be God's tool to do something eternal in the heart of the person who has hurt you most. When we have been wounded, terribly wounded, we want to do something drastic in return. At the very least, we want to unload a scalding tirade to vent our anger. What God requires of us is a reply that will be "full of grace, seasoned with salt." That simply means the words we use must help to do what salt does—heal and preserve and make palatable.

After Corrie ten Boom was released from a German concentration camp, she felt the need to write to the person who had betrayed her family to the Nazis. It was not only a

letter of forgiveness, but one designed to bring this perpetrator of such evil to the Savior:

Haarlem, June 19, 1945

Dear Sir,

*Today I heard that most probably you are the one
who betrayed me. I went through ten months of concentration camp. My father died after nine days of
imprisonment. My sister died in prison too.*

*The harm you planned was turned into good for me
by God. I came nearer to Him. A severe punishment
is awaiting you. I have prayed for you, that the Lord
may accept you if you will repent. Think that the
Lord Jesus on the Cross also took your sins upon
Himself. If you accept this and want to be His child,
you are saved for eternity.*

*I have forgiven you everything. God will also for-
give you everything if you ask Him. He loves you and
He Himself sent His Son to earth to reconcile your
sins, which meant to suffer the punishment for you
and me. You on your part have to give an answer to
this. If He says, "Come unto Me, give Me your heart,"
then your answer must be, "Yes, Lord, I come, make
me Your child." If it is difficult for you to pray, then
ask if God will give you His Spirit, who works the
faith in your heart.*

*Never doubt the Lord Jesus' love. He is standing
with His arms spread out to receive you.*

*I hope that the path which you will now take may
work for your eternal salvation.*

CORRIE TEN BOOM[3]

You will notice that Corrie ten Boom never said, "What
you did really wasn't so bad." She made it clear how deep
the hurt had been, but she did not stop there. She gave

her own forgiveness and she gave something even better—
the offer of God's forgiveness as well.

Perhaps there is no way in which we can act more like
Christ than when we dare to forgive what seems unforgivable!

NINE

FORGIVENESS AND THE CHARACTER OF GOD

I f you could "design" a perfect God, what would He be like? Such a question sounds sacrilegious and foolish, but stay with me!

Such a God would have to be powerful enough to fix any problem, wise enough to understand not only all the known facts in the universe, but the unknown and undreamed-of ones as well; He would have to be completely unchanging, absolutely reliable. Of course, He would have to be a God of justice and righteousness, or how could there ever be *any* goodness in the universe? And obviously, He would have to be a God of mercy too, because justice without mercy would be a pretty hopeless prospect.

You get my point. That's the kind of God we have!

But even as essential as these attributes are for all of us frail, faltering human beings in need of a great and powerful God who is also righteous and fair and merciful, we need more. We need a God who not only knows our behavior, good and bad, but who also sees into the very depths of our hearts and knows *why* we behave the way we do. More importantly, we require a God who is able to fix the problems of the heart and who cares enough about us to do just that!

When we are struggling with life's deepest issues, the

holiness and glory and power of God have to be expressed
in a way that makes a difference where we live—not simply as part of an abstract list of the attributes of the Eternal God. And that is exactly what God does for us!

When our son Jim was a tiny little boy, his grandfather
gave him a toy electric razor for his birthday. Of course, it
did nothing but make a loud noise, but Jimmy was very
proud of it and he used it to "shave" with his dad every
morning.

One day, the battery slipped out of place and the razor
would not work. My husband and I both offered to fix it,
but Jimmy was determined to take it to "Pawpaw" to be
repaired.

I knew how busy Jimmy's granddad was, but I also
knew he loved to have his grandchildren visit the office, so
Jimmy and I drove to see him. When we arrived, Jimmy
did not check in with the secretary for an appointment,
even though others were waiting. Instead, he burst into his
grandfather's office and ran straight into the arms of his
beloved "Pawpaw." It didn't matter that an important
meeting was going on. Jimmy's grandfather stopped everything long enough to fix the razor, to offer a piece of
candy, and to show Jimmy the new fish in the aquarium.
Then with a final kiss and hug, he waved good-bye.

To be a child of God, dearly loved and planned for, and
yet to see Him only in the formal setting of His might and
glory in the universe would be a tragedy! Such a relationship would be less comprehensible than the thought of a
grandfather who found no pleasure in the presence of his
own grandson.

And yet that is the way many of God's children do view
Him. They acknowledge that He is a force to be reckoned
with; and they struggle, often valiantly, to be what they ought
to be, in order to avoid being "zapped" by this God whose
demands are so difficult to meet! But because their view of
His character is so limited, they never feel totally forgiven
and therefore do not know how to forgive other people.

GOD'S TENDERNESS

Perhaps no characteristic of our Great God is so greatly underestimated as His tenderness. At one of the most distressing points in the history of the Jewish nation, with foreign armies setting up camp at the very walls of Jerusalem, God reminded His people over and over again that although they had turned their backs on Him, He would never let them go. "In all their distress He too was distressed" (Isaiah 63:9).

Only a perfect God could find a way to reconcile such tenderness with His unchanging justice and righteousness and hatred of evil. No one but God could display the love expressed in the promise, "For a brief moment I abandoned you, but with deep compassion I will bring you back. In a surge of anger I hid my face from you for a moment, but with everlasting kindness I will have compassion on you" (Isaiah 54:7-8).

Most of us would feel a need to let our anger run its course; few of us would consider telling the one who had grieved us deeply that our anger was only momentary, and that our compassion and forgiveness would be forever! But that is the kind of God we have!

1. God's tender touch. I suspect that all of us show our greatest tenderness in relationship to small children. We are constantly aware of their vulnerability and their dependence, and we want to protect them. It is not surprising, then, that God uses this illustration of His love and care for His own: "As a father has compassion on his children, so the Lord has compassion on those who fear Him; for He knows how we are formed, He remembers that we are dust" (Psalm 103:13-14).

The catch word here is *remember*.

Psalm 78:38-39 says further, "Time after time He restrained His anger and did not stir up His full wrath. He remembered that they were but flesh."

God can love us, incomplete and failing as we are, because He knows where we came from. His expectations match His knowledge of what we are.

2. God's tender thoughts. One of the most amazing elements of God's relationship to His own children is that He delights in thinking about us and planning for our welfare.

In Psalm 139:17-18 the psalmist says, "How precious to me [or *concerning me*] are Your thoughts, O God! How vast is the sum of them! Were I to count them, they would outnumber the grains of sand. When I awake, I am still with You." In Jeremiah 29:11 God speaks to the Children of Israel in the desperate certainty of their captivity, but He speaks to all of us as well who may feel we are in a hopeless situation, "I know the plans (also translated *thoughts*) I have for you . . . plans to prosper you and not to harm you, plans to give you a hope and a future."

3. God as a tender tutor. No part of childrearing is as difficult as discipline, and I use that word in its broadest sense—not simply in the area of punishment for wrongdoing, but rather in terms of instruction in righteousness, in development of character. The problem is that we have a hard time picturing present temporary pain as an indication of a parent's tender regard for his child's future.

But God sees the cause and effect, the present and the future better than we do, and His discipline in our lives is not contrary to, but in exact proportion to, His love for us! In Hebrews 12:5-11 we read:

> *My son, do not make light of the Lord's discipline, and do not lose heart when He rebukes you, because the Lord disciplines those He loves, and He punishes everyone He accepts as a son. . . . Our fathers disciplined us for a little while as they thought best; but God disciplines us for our good, that we may share in His holiness. No discipline seems pleasant at the time, but painful. Later on, however, it produces a harvest of righteousness and peace for those who have been trained by it.*

*Although the Lord gives you the bread of adversity
and the water of affliction, your teachers will be hidden no more; with your own eyes you will see them.
Whether you turn to the right or to the left, your ears
will hear a voice behind you saying, "This is the way;
walk in it" (Isaiah 30:20-21).*

A young mother, whose small children were perpetually
out of control, was challenged by a teacher to make serious effort to alter their behavior. "It isn't just that they are
a 'pain in the neck' to other people; their own ability to be
properly educated is at stake!" the teacher said.

"I know," the young mother said with a sigh. "It's just
that I love them too much to discipline them!"

God is not so misguided about love. He loves us enough
to want the very best for us, and it is His tender concern
for us that demands the lessons of adversity.

4. God as a tender taskmaster. When Adam and Eve
sinned in the Garden of Eden, part of the curse was that
man's survival would depend upon his own hard work:

*Cursed is the ground because of you; through painful
toil you will eat of it all the days of your life. It will
produce thorns and thistles for you, and you will eat
the plants of the field. By the sweat of your brow you
will eat your food until you return to the ground,
since from it you were taken; for dust you are and to
dust you will return (Genesis 3:17-19).*

In the *King James Version,* the phrase "because of you"
reads "for your sake," and my own impression is that it
may be more in keeping with God's intent. Like all the
elements of the curse, God planned that evil could be a
way for Him to demonstrate His power over the effects of
sin.

Our technological skills and gifts have gone far in modifying and refining the "painful toil" which was part of the

curse, but we will never be able to completely eliminate the necessity for hard work.

But, consistent with the character of God, He does not leave us to struggle alone; He has promised to "share the load" as a tender taskmaster.

In Matthew 11:28-30 we read this invitation, "Come to Me, all you who are weary and burdened, and I will give you rest. Take My yoke upon you and learn from Me, for I am gentle and humble in heart, and you will find rest for your souls. For My yoke is easy and My burden is light."

Isaiah 40:31 also reminds us of the source of our strength, "Those who hope in the Lord will renew their strength. They will soar on wings like eagles; they will run and not grow weary; and they will walk and not be faint."

Especially for those who work hard in their ministry for the Lord and for other people, these words from Hebrews 6:10 have application, "God is not unjust; He will not forget your work and the love you have shown Him as you have helped His people and continue to help them."

5. God's tender tears. Does it seem strange to you to think of God weeping? We know that Jesus wept at the death of Lazarus, but there were also tears when He looked out over the city of Jerusalem and saw the rejection of those He loved and longed to bring to Himself.

One of the most beautiful human pictures of God is that of the father in the Parable of the Prodigal Son. Even while the son was a great way off, "his father saw him, and had compassion, and ran, and fell on his neck, and kissed him" (Luke 15:20, KJV). Perhaps a modern interpretation of the phrase "fell on his neck" would be that the man threw his arms around his son, but I do not think it would be a false assumption to say that the prodigal son's father wept over him. Would we misrepresent the character of God if we said that He weeps over His children who have gone astray?

Even now the Holy Spirit weeps as He prays for us. In Romans 8:26-27 we read:

In the same way, the Spirit helps us in our weakness. We do not know what we ought to pray for, but the Spirit Himself intercedes for us with groans that words cannot express. And He who searches our hearts knows the mind of the Spirit, because the Spirit intercedes for the saints in accordance with God's will.

TENDERNESS SEEN THROUGH A GLASS DARKLY

Why is the tenderness of God so hard for us to comprehend? Perhaps it is because we do not know how to view God beyond the limitations of our own frailties and finite understanding. We do not have the range of God's thoughts; we cannot see our lives in the scope of eternity.

In her little book, *Pain: The Gift Nobody Wants*, my late sister, Grace MacMullen, related her own poignant insight into the heart of God:

Our daugther, Allana, is deaf. In the State of Idaho where we lived there was just one school for deaf children, a residential school forty miles away. Just a few weeks after she turned four, she was accepted into the school in Gooding. She could not hear or talk, and at that time knew no signs. It was her only chance for an education, but how could we give her up?

We got her ready for the trip, unable to tell her where we were going or why. She packed gaily, for she loved traveling, but became quiet when she saw the rest of the family had no suitcases.

As we brought up her clothes and pointed to the small bed that was to be hers, she became more and more anxious and distressed. Finally she whimpered and held on to us, and then began to cry. We felt our hearts break. We could not say, 'We love you. We'll be back in a couple of weeks. You'll be home this

summer.' It seemed to her we were abandoning her
to strangers for some unfathomable reason. There
was no way she could know she would ever see us
again. To the pain and loneliness was added the
grief of not understanding why this awful thing had
to be done.

Fighting back the overwhelming tears, we loos-
ened her clutching arms, gave her to the dormitory
supervisor, and cruelly, callously, she thought, we
walked out the door.

It was perhaps the most completely unselfish,
greatest act of love we ever did for her. Painful as it
was to her, it was also heartbreaking for us.

So I am sure God must also sometimes wipe away
a tear of sympathy for our struggles, saying, "I wish
you could see the reasons now, but you can't."[1]

All of us, like little Allana, come to those times in our
lives when nothing we see happening around us fits our
picture of what life is supposed to be like. People we trusted have let us down; cherished dreams are destroyed by
someone's selfishness or greed; our sense of security is
disturbed by the evils we see in society.

We learn quickly that we can't depend on others!

I was a college girl, and very much in love. I had been
dating a young man who was the epitome of everything I
wanted in a husband. He was talented, popular, musical,
well-dressed, active in Christian service, and interested in
all the things that interested me. It seemed that he was
going to be the answer to my prayers!

But one day, not long before graduation, the relationship ended. I was heartbroken and in a letter to my dad, I
shared the sense of loss and disappointment I felt. This
was his reply:

It would be well for you to have whatever training
the blessed Savior knows you need, to ripen your

*heart and make it humble, and make it appreciative
and make your vision large and your charity and
sympathy great. For I tell you now, there is no way to
learn to know about other people's hurts, and to help
carry their burdens, like having your own heart
broken.*

*On this matter I thank God as I have for long years,
that He has taught me the meaning of suffering. I
know how to comfort every orphan child, because I
was an orphan. I know how to fellowship with the
poorest of the poor; I have been as poor as any of
them were. I know how to be a friend to those who
are demeaned and slandered. . . . Bruises and hurts
are sad for the moment, but like all chastisement
from the hand of God, they afterward work "the
peaceable fruit of righteousness." God is too good to
ever allow a pain that does not mean a blessing.[2]*

Dad was right. Life can be understood only through a
clear picture of the nature and character of God. If we
assume that whatever comes to us is in direct relationship
to God's love for us, we will not get hung up on the source
of our pain. If we really believe that God is using the failure of someone else as a tool in our lives for building
righteousness, then we can forgive what may even seem to
be unforgivable.

When things go well and days are bright, it is good to be
reminded that we have a gracious, loving God who delights in giving His children things that are pleasant and
good.

But when we are in dire need, where loved ones are
desperately ill, when our livelihood is taken from us, when
circumstances or people have blocked the work we believe
God has given us to do, then it is good to know that our
God is a God of power who can use all the resources of
heaven and earth for the needs of His own dear children.

When we have sinned and disgraced the name of the

Lord and brought damage to our own reputation and character, how wonderful to know that we have a God of mercy and grace—One who forgives the penitent sinner and who removes and forgets forever the foul and filthy thoughts and actions of His contrite child.

When we have been mistreated, lied about, and misjudged, it is good to know we have a God who is fair and just—One who sees the motives of the heart and knows how to deal out retribution and correction and vengeance in perfect degree and timing.

When nothing in life seems to make sense, when the wicked seem to prosper and the righteous seem to have more than their share of suffering, when we are confused and disillusioned and perplexed, it is so important to know that we have a God whose wisdom is far beyond what any human mind can comprehend. Our rest of heart must come through an acceptance of the fact that God is not required to explain to us His dealings with us. We must humbly acknowledge that even if He chose to tell us how He was working out His will in the affairs of this world, we would not have the capacity to fully understand.

Ultimately, life has no meaning, and the problems of the world have no solution, apart from God. How important it is, then, that we *know* Him—not simply His promises or His commands but His very character and nature, His relationship to those who have made Him Lord and Savior.

TEN

IS FORGIVENESS
ALWAYS INSTANT
AND PERMANENT?

You have seen them—the bag ladies—walking the streets of any major city. Their hair is matted and uncombed; their faces are brown and lined with care and exposure. They pick through garbage and pile the bits and pieces of other peoples' junk on stolen shopping carts or hoard them like hidden treasure in old grocery sacks.

Summer or winter they wear layers of dirty and tattered clothing which they dare not discard; it will be their bedding when night comes.

They live only in the present, without past or future.

They have lost a sense of what is valuable and what is not.

They live without awareness of available resources; they depend only on themselves.

They have nothing to give to others; they are concerned only with getting their own needs met.

They are often in pain, addicted, and lonely.

They trust no one; their wary eyes reflect a disillusionment with a society that has rejected them and let them down.

They are lost to the system, often living outside its laws and its protection.

Who are these women and why do they live as they do?

SPIRITUAL BAG LADIES

We are repulsed and shocked and saddened at the sight of such hopelessness. We are puzzled at the idea that a woman may become so estranged from family and friends, so beyond the resources of society that she sleeps over a sidewalk heating vent and clings desperately to a pitiful collection of junk!

Depressing as the picture may be, it is possible that some of us are like spiritual bag ladies—clutching our hurt and anger and unforgiveness to our breasts as though it were the only thing that gave us significance.

The mentality is easy to identify:

"I made a fool of myself once," the spiritual bag lady says. "I threw away my love on somebody who treated me like dirt. You just see if I ever let that happen again!"

"My kids never appreciated a thing I did for them. What's the use of having children anyway? They just break your heart."

"The people at that church never met my needs. I can do without 'em!"

"Well, I've found out you just can't trust anybody. Everyone's busy looking out for number one!"

If you heard your own voice in any of the above comments, you may need to open the garbage sack and unload the junk!

We never start out intending to be emotional garbage collectors. But then the first disappointment came, when someone we loved and trusted let us down. It may be that we had expectations of others that never could have been met; perhaps the damage was inflicted out of insensitivity and selfishness, or worse yet, deliberate malice.

If that injury was not handled properly—acknowledged, challenged, and then forgiven—we put a little mark in our mental "grudge books" and determined we wouldn't let that person disappoint us again.

If our response was one of simply "letting bygones be

bygones," without any decisive plan of dealing with the anger and disappointment, we probably felt pretty good about the way we had handled the problem until that person, or someone else we loved and trusted, hurt us again and again. By then, the "grudge book" seemed to be the only way we could protect ourselves from pain!

How can we get rid of our excess baggage—the anger, the bitterness, the accumulated garbage of our unforgiveness? And what do we do when we have been hurt in such an unspeakable way that we feel we may never be able to trust people again?

"Quick forgiveness" is not the answer. To lightly dismiss any grievance which stirs us to deep anger is not helpful. It doesn't give us a sense of "finished business," and it doesn't correct the problem that may have required forgiveness in the first place! Even when our response is far more emotional than the situation warranted, we need to take time to look at the sources of our anger and do whatever it takes to be able to write in our hearts, "Account closed."

For those who recognize in themselves a tendency to misread every gesture and look and word of others, and to assume that there is a grievance or malicious intent in every daily contact, the issue is not even one of forgiveness but of perception. Those who suspect evil in every family member or acquaintance are, indeed, bag ladies, but forgiveness will not help them. They must learn first to see themselves as loved and valued by God, and therefore as valuable to others.

But what if there *has* been identifiable sin committed that has hurt us terribly? We tried to forgive and wanted to forgive, but we find that in spite of everything, the garbage bag hasn't been discarded. We can't let it go.

It may be that forgiveness has never "worked" because it was too immediate; it was what some have called "cheap" forgiveness. Offenses that are lightly brushed off as "no big deal" are rarely settled permanently.

1. First, forgiveness requires facing all the facts. Instant forgiveness may mask or short-circuit a deeper problem not apparent on the surface. When you forgive, make sure you know exactly what it is you have to forgive.

2. Genuine forgiveness requires time to acknowledge anger. To pretend one is not hurt or angry, in an attempt to accomplish forgiveness and restore a relationship quickly, will only give opportunity for anger to turn into a smoldering bitterness. Be honest in facing what you feel.

3. Forgiveness should not minimize the offender's need to express his guilt and sorrow at the offense. Confession is important for the one who has sinned; a quick forgiveness which shortcuts this painful process is no kindness to the perpetrator.

4. Forgiveness should always be administered in the clear understanding of what expectations are involved.

Does the one who has been hurt assume that forgiveness will "keep this thing from happening again?" Not necessarily!

Does the offender assume that instant forgiveness proves "this wasn't such a bad thing I did?" Wrong!

Forgiveness needs to be deliberate enough and thoughtful enough that both parties know exactly what it means. Biblical forgiveness has no conditions, but this openness is extremely difficult to accomplish when we forgive "too soon."

ELEMENTS OF PROGRESSIVE FORGIVENESS

Progressive forgiveness is not the same thing as delayed forgiveness or withheld forgiveness. It does not "play games" with the offender as a way of producing repentance.

Progressive forgiveness always begins with a *determination* to forgive. It proceeds on the understanding that forgiveness is a choice rather than a feeling.

Possible steps in progressive forgiveness:

1. Pray, "Lord, I want to be obedient to Your will. Show

me how to deal with this offense in such a way that You will be glorified."

2. Be willing to say to the offender, "I am feeling very angry about what has happened, and I am hurt because it feels as though you didn't care how this would wound me. I value our relationship and I choose to forgive, but I need to work through the way I feel."

3. Allow time for examination of the offense:

"What was this person thinking?"

"Is there more about this I need to know?"

"Are there other people involved in this offense?"

"Is this part of a pattern? Is there an addiction involved?"

"Do I really understand what has happened and what may have precipitated it?"

"How does God fit into all of this?"

"Is there something that may come out later that could hurt me further?"

Especially in the case of marital infidelity, it might not be helpful to seek or to tell every intimate element of an affair—actions or feelings. If, however, there are details that have already been exposed in some public way, or if there are repercussions that are likely to occur later, the one who has been hurt should have full disclosure. Otherwise, the injury of hearing facts from someone else may be worse than the original offense.

4. Set aside time for working through the pain and anger that has come as a result of the offense.

Begin with God. Thank Him for the way He has forgiven you in all your offenses. Check out all the Scriptures that will remind you of the magnitude of your own offenses, and the marvel of God's forgiveness. Apply Ephesians 2:1-5 to your own heart:

> As for you, you were dead in your transgressions and sins, in which you used to live when you followed the ways of this world and of the ruler of the kingdom of the air, the spirit who is now at work in those who

are disobedient. All of us also lived among them at one time, gratifying the cravings of our sinful nature and following its desires and thoughts. Like the rest, we were by nature objects of wrath. But because of His great love for us, God, who is rich in mercy, made us alive with Christ even when we were dead in transgressions—it is by grace you have been saved.

Ask God to help you respond to the one who has hurt you in the same way Jesus Christ responded to you:

May the God who gives endurance and encouragement give you a spirit of unity among yourselves as you follow Christ Jesus, so that with one heart and mouth you may glorify the God and Father of our Lord Jesus Christ. Accept one another, then, just as Christ accepted you, in order to bring praise to God (Romans 15:5-7).

Don't be afraid to identify your reactions. Sometimes a child of God will assume, incorrectly, that the only proper response to hurt is to bury negative feelings. To deny or suppress the pain of having been offended will only create greater problems later. We cannot deal with anything we have not identified.

A more healthy approach would be to actually list on paper the emotional responses we feel:

confusion?	hopelessness?
despair?	humiliation?
shame?	loneliness?
fury?	

Once we have dared to face "the monsters in the closet," we can turn them over to God one by one to be healed and forgiven and erased.

One woman who had been hurt by the unfaithfulness of her minister-husband wrote:

*I was so furious at what happened that I was literally
shaking. I had never felt such immense anger, but I
wasn't sure who I was mad at. I finally found myself
writing on a piece of paper:*

*I am angry at myself that I allowed some things to
occur unchallenged.*

*I am angry at people who have taken advantage of
my submission.*

*I am angry at my husband that my love and repu-
tation could be taken so lightly.*

*I am angry at God for allowing these things to
happen.*

God is not shocked by what we feel or write down.
He already knows more about our feelings than we do
ourselves. When we have acknowledged the darkest
thoughts from the depths of our innermost being, then
we can take them to Him for cleansing and healing.

*For we do not have a high priest who is unable to
sympathize with our weaknesses, but we have One
who has been tempted in every way, just as we are—
yet was without sin. Let us then approach the throne
of grace with confidence, so that we may receive
mercy and find grace to help us in our time of need
(Hebrews 4:15-16).*

At some point, in the midst of our pain and heartache, every one of us must learn to hold out our
hands to God (with all those things we are clutching—whatever we consider essential to our happiness) and give Him the right to do with us as He
pleases. It is a right He already possesses, but relinquishing our claim to ourselves will free us to forgive
those we may feel have damaged our happiness.

5. Recognize the possible necessity of forgiving over
and over again, as "layers of the onion" are revealed:

Memories triggered by unexpected stimuli: pictures, anniversaries, holidays, a casual remark, a song. Sometimes when we think the book is closed and forgiveness is complete, a sudden reminder of that thing which happened overwhelms and confuses; we experience again the hurt and anger that we thought was permanently discarded. When that happens, we must go back, not to the one who hurt us to open old wounds, but to the One who has the instant prescription—that balm in Gilead that brought healing the first time we needed it.

Revelation of more facts. A woman who discovered her husband's receipts for several nights' lodging in a local motel confronted him with her suspicions. He acknowledged, with tears, that he had been unfaithful to her, but insisted it was not a "love" relationship. He convinced her of his love for her and she forgave him. It was not a step she took lightly, and it was, as far as she knew, total forgiveness. When she later discovered that the young woman with whom her husband had been involved was pregnant, it was a major blow to the relationship. She had genuinely forgiven and had never made an attempt to hold the affair over her husband's head, but now she found that she would have to go through the process of forgiveness at a different level.

Times of discouragement or depression. Satan loves to use our "down" times to remind us of how badly we have been wounded by other people. How easily he leads us through dark tunnels of our memories when we are already discouraged! If we are not careful, all the evil deeds ever done against us, all the spiteful responses we have ever heard, will float to the top in the Slough of Despond! We need a pre-planned system for dealing with remembered offenses when we are depressed: First, to forgive again (within our own hearts), then to replace what is dark with what is light—perhaps using one single blessed promise from the Word which we have reserved for this very occasion. We may have to remind ourselves of the conditions for rest of heart as given in Psalm 119:165, "Great peace have they which love Thy law, and *nothing* shall offend them" (KJV).

Repeated offenses. Here's the tough one! How often forgiveness must be repeated over and over again in households where there is a problem with alcohol or other addictions!

Most of us think of forgiveness in terms of what one has *done*. For a person who is addicted, forgiveness must be in terms of what one *is*. It is always easier to forgive the act than the condition! But God's forgiveness extends far beyond what each one of us *did*, or *will* do, for that matter. God forgives us for what we ARE! And so there is a sense in which one who forgives an alcoholic gets more opportunity to behave like God. Forgiveness has to be administered on a daily basis.

Having said that, we need to remember that forgiveness is not the same thing as aiding and abetting what is wrong! Forgiving one who struggles with repeated offenses does not mean we sit idly by, allowing the problem to continue without any intervention on our part. Here again, we must not only forgive as God forgives; we must love as God loves. And God loves enough to want the very best for us. God often practices "tough love" and we must practice it too.

This may require our coming to the point of saying, "Enough is enough. I will not allow you to go on this way unchallenged. I will make whatever sacrifices are required to get help for you and I will run down every resource I can find, but I will not sit quietly and allow your life to continue in this way."

Such a stand is always difficult, sometimes nearly impossible. But we have a right to assume that God is as concerned as we are, and that He can do in the lives of our loved ones what we cannot do.

WHAT IS COMPLETE FORGIVENESS?

1. Forgiveness is complete when we refuse to keep bringing up the offense of the one who has hurt us.

2. Forgiveness is complete when our eyes, our words, our touch, and our thoughts express love, not condemnation.

3. Forgiveness is complete when we have learned to live in the present and future instead of the past.

4. Forgiveness is complete when we have relinquished our expectations for the one who has hurt us.

5. Forgiveness is complete when we have activated a plan for rechanneling memories of pain—"bringing into captivity every thought to the obedience of Christ."

6. Forgiveness is complete when we discover within ourselves a steady awareness of our own gracious forgiveness at the hand of God.

In her little book *Lord, It Keeps Happening . . . and Happening*, Ruth Harms Calkins expresses the struggle many of us feel:

MORBID MEMORIES

Lord, I can't mow down morbid memories
Like my husband mows tall grass.
Mercilessly they take revenge
By tramping gleefully
Through my somber heart.
So, dear Lord,
I ask YOU to shake them
In the sunlight of Your love.
Then may the gentle breeze
of the Holy Spirit
Blow them all away—
Never to be found again.[1]

Some have said that forgiveness is not complete until the person who was hurt has totally forgotten what happened. Short of one acquiring amnesia, I do not believe that is possible.

In many cases, the offense is so intertwined with other things happening at that moment in time that it can never be entirely forgotten. But when forgiveness is complete, the memory evokes not terrible pain or anger, but rather a new reminder of God's healing power.

When Jesus was comforting His disciples about His coming death on the cross, He gave this illustration:

> *You will grieve, but your grief will turn to joy. A woman giving birth to a child has pain because her time has come; but when her baby is born she forgets the anguish because of her joy that a child is born into the world. So with you: Now is your time of grief, but I will see you again and you will rejoice, and no one will take away your joy (John 16:20-22).*

A woman who has a baby does not forget that she *had* pain; her memory of it is simply colored by her joy in the new baby!

And so it must be that the memories of past acknowledged sin—our own or others'—must be colored by the glory of the grace of God.

> *Therefore, since we have been justified through faith, we have peace with God through our Lord Jesus Christ, through whom we have gained access by faith into this grace in which we now stand. And we rejoice in the hope of the glory of God. Not only so, but we also rejoice in our sufferings, because we know that suffering produces perseverance; perseverance, character; and character, hope. And hope*

does not disappoint us, because God has poured out
His love into our hearts by the Holy Spirit, whom He
has given us (Romans 5:1-5).

With all the resources of heaven at our disposal, it would be a shame for any of us to behave as spiritual bag ladies—carting around all the bitterness and unforgiveness of the past. Begin today to let it all go! Take out the garbage!

ELEVEN

WORDS! WORDS! WORDS! WHY FORGIVENESS MUST BE VERBAL

---

magine, if you can, all the sounds of the universe, from the beginning of creation, spinning around somewhere out in space:

Every laugh.
Every blast from a cannon.
Every whisper of love.
Every clap of thunder.
Every birdsong.
Every sigh.
Every scream.
Every melody.

Several years ago a popular scientist whose articles often appeared in the Sunday papers, suggested just such a possibility. Perhaps, he said, sound waves never really dissipate but merely keep moving in space.

What if sound really *is* permanent? What if every angry word, every cruel remark, every shouted insult, really is whirling around out there somewhere between the planets?

Pretty sobering thought, isn't it? If we really believed that to be true, most of us would work a lot harder at sweetening the airwaves!

There is a sense in which words *are* permanent. Jesus made this clear to the hypocritical Pharisees:

For out of the overflow of the heart the mouth speaks. The good man brings good things out of the good stored up in him, and the evil man brings evil things out of the evil stored up in him. But I tell you that men will have to give account on the day of judgment for every careless word they have spoken. For by your words you will be acquitted, and by your words, you will be condemned (Matthew 12:34-37).

What a prospect! When our self-control slips and we end up hurting a person we love by some outrageous outburst, we make excuses for ourselves by saying, "Well, you know me! I always say things I don't really mean!"

We hope people will simply dismiss the cutting accusations and forget we ever said them, but they don't!

Words that hurt have a way of building a nest deep in the heart of the one who was wounded. Not only are the actual words remembered, the very facial expression and the angry physical stance are also buried in the memory.

But of more serious consequence, our words will be judged by the God of the universe, who also hears!

If there is any way at all that words can be erased from our memory tapes, it will be through the process of confession and forgiveness.

Someone has said that the two hardest things to say are, "I love you," and "I'm sorry. I was wrong." Many people struggle with the inability to say, "I love you," but almost everybody finds it difficult to say, "I was wrong."

While God does not give us the privilege of limiting our forgiveness only to those who have admitted their blame, we should give opportunity and encouragement for the offender to sincerely apologize. Of course, we can't *make* people say the right things that will accomplish healing in the best way; but we do have a right to say to the one who has hurt us, "I need you to understand how much this has hurt. Just hearing you say 'I'm sorry' would certainly help."

It isn't particularly helpful if the person who has offended says, "I couldn't help it (because of my past, other people, the devil, etc.)."

"I didn't mean it to be as bad as it sounded."

"If you had been there for me."

"Everybody has this problem."

In fact, we are not particularly comforted if the person who has offended us says, "Well, I'm sorry *if* I hurt you." We want to know that there is a sense of genuine sorrow because of what was said or done.

In Psalm 51, David's great model prayer of confession after his adultery with Bathsheba and subsequent murder of Uriah, we can see clearly the losses that come with unconfessed sin:

1. Loss of a good conscience. "My sin is ever before me."

2. Loss of joy and gladness. "Let me hear joy and gladness; let the bones You have crushed rejoice."

3. Loss of the presence of God. "Do not cast me from your presence or take Your Holy Spirit from me."

The positive side of all the pain that comes with unconfessed sin is that it is curable! As David Augsburger says, "We discover and experience release from our guilt in direct proportion to our willingness to face our sin, confess our sinfulness and accept forgiveness. We must 'turn ourselves in.' "[1]

WHAT IS THE PROCESS OF CONFESSION?

1. Confession should begin by laying out our sin before God, knowing that He is the only One who has power to heal and to free us from the guilt of our wrongdoing. As Lloyd Ogilvie writes:

We are to forget the past by remembering the Lord.
We are to remember He has forgotten our sins and
failures. And yet, we must confess them specifically

if we are to be healed. At His command we are to march through the prison of our memories, leading out each captive memory for display before Him. We are urged to state our own case against ourselves and then be acquitted. All of our mistakes and all the injustices that have wounded us must be brought into the court of His presence. Then as we finish our condemnatory judgment on ourselves and others He says, "I forgot that long ago; now you are free to forget it."[2]

2. Working through some sins of the past may require sharing with a trusted friend. David Seamands writes:

We talk a lot about being honest with ourselves and with God. And we sincerely—sometimes desperately—try to do this in our times of Bible reading and prayer. But the kind of honesty and self-knowledge which will bring about lasting changes in our lives almost always requires another person. It is when we disclose our true, private selves to someone else that we fully come to know ourselves for real. Down deep we may simply perceive the truth about our real selves, yet go on denying or covering it with our superselves—even in prayer. However, once we have actually put the truth into words and shared with another, it becomes increasingly difficult to continue deceiving ourselves.[3]

Protestants have been wary of the confessional booth; however, we all *do* need a safe and healthy environment within the church body that allows for confession of sin. James 5:16 says, "Confess your sins to each other and pray for each other, so that you may be healed. The prayer of a righteous man is powerful and effective."

Whether you enjoy the fellowship of a small "accountability group" or have a prayer partner or feel the freedom of talking with a Sunday School teacher or church staff member, make sure you have *some-one* in your life who will help you to be honest with yourself.

3. Ask forgiveness of the one you have wounded. Whatever the circumstance that precipitated the problem, use no excuses when you ask forgiveness. Painful as it may be to say the words, state simply what you did that was wrong, and then tell the person you hurt how sorry you are for what you did. Gary Rosberg warns:

> It isn't enough to say, "Okay, if you think I did some-thing wrong, let's talk about it." Nor is it appropriate to say, "I don't think I did anything that was such a big deal, but since you think I did, let's talk." We need to confront the wrongdoing: "I am wrong." "What I did to you is wrong." "I have done wrong and I need to talk to you about what I did to offend."[4]

Is there ever a time when sins should not be con-fessed to anyone except God?

Probably.

In a marriage, when there has been sexual sin in the past which has been forsaken, forgiven by God, and has little likelihood of ever coming to the knowl-edge of the marriage partner, it might be an act of kindness not to reveal it to a mate who is particularly fragile emotionally or spiritually.

> If you should choose not to confess, for the sake of being most redemptive and loving to the other person, be aware that you are choosing the harder, not the easier way. To live with the unshared memo-ry of your sin, to find forgiveness without sharing the meaning of that forgiveness, is not an easier way. It

is all the more demanding, of you and your own spir-
itual and emotional maturity. This is true, because
essentially, confession is a human necessity.[5]

In the fellowship of believers, we must be careful not to encourage a kind of pietistic voyeurism by a public revelation and discussion of sexual sins. Even when details have already become common knowledge, it seems to me that public confession should include only the simplest humble statement that one has broken God's commandment and hurt others and therefore seeks forgiveness and reestablishing of fellowship within the body of Christ.

If we equate "proper repentance" with a lurid description of all the evil thoughts and actions involved in the sin, then we are presuming to take the place of God. Only God can measure the quantity and quality of repentance. And I suspect that in our churches, we could do a better job of thwarting the devices of Satan by avoiding the gossip and speculations that often accompany a confession of sin. Sometimes we pass on information in the form of "prayer requests" that may, in fact, be incorrect and permanently damaging. When we later discover our knowledge to be inaccurate, the feathers have been scattered too far to be retrieved; a reputation has been forever tarnished.

If we are to "bear each other's burdens" and "confess our faults to each other," there has to be a personal integrity in the way these are shared and received.

HOW TO RESPOND TO A CONFESSION OF SIN

When the difficult and struggling words of confession have finally been spoken, then God holds the wounded party accountable for the way he responds. We are tempted to blurt out, "How could you have done this to me?" Obviously such a response would not be helpful. That person who has come to the place of acknowledging sin probably wonders himself how such a wound could have been inflicted. Not one of us knows our own heart; we do not understand why we do what we do.

Still, there are questions that can and perhaps should be asked;

"Do you want to tell me your side of the story?"

"Do you understand why I feel so hurt about this?"

"Is there anything I can do to keep this problem from occurring between us again?"

But finally, the healing words must be spoken,

"I forgive you."

"I value our relationship and I want to do my part in restoring it, if possible."

"I recognize how culpable we all are before God. I am having to work on my problems too."

"I forgive you and I will not drag this out in front of you again. It is over."

If there is to be any discussion at all following the request for forgiveness, it should be only what will help to restore the relationship and bring healing.

There are times when saying, "I forgive you," is inappropriate.

"I'm really floored," my friend Kay said to me the other day. "A lady in the church just said to me, 'I want you to know I've forgiven you for what you did to me back in November.' "

Kay had such a puzzled look on her face I had to smile. "Just what was this thing you did to her back in November?" I asked.

"I haven't the slightest idea! I was so taken off guard that I didn't even think to ask! I've thought and thought and can't come up with anything."

Perhaps the lady thought she was fulfilling, in some sort of a backward way, Jesus' command in

Matthew 5:23-24: "If you are offering your gift at the altar and there remember that your brother has something against you, leave your gift there in front of the altar. First go and be reconciled to your brother; then come and offer your gift."

I rather expect Kay to go back to the "forgiver of the unknown sin" to make further inquiries about the nature of the problem. Then if she really does need to say, "I'm sorry," she will know it.

But the real issue here has to do with our motives in "giving" forgiveness. The point of forgiveness is to heal a broken relationship. If I announce to someone that I have forgiven him for an offense I have never identified, or suggest that I want to restore a relationship the offender never even knew was broken, is it possible I am working on a hidden agenda? Am I secretly hoping to produce guilt? Do I view this act as a mark of spiritual superiority?

Maybe, in all honesty, I am genuinely trying to clear the air because I still feel myself to be holding a grudge for something that happened a long time ago.

Sometimes, we have to leave unspoken the words of forgiveness we feel in our hearts. Instead, we must carry them to the throne of grace and say to the Heavenly Father, "This thing that happened so long ago still bothers me and I know I must let it go. And so, Lord, I bring my gift of forgiveness to You. I will allow You to wipe out the differences that have hurt this relationship. I will behave as though the relationship were in perfect order."

WHY WORDS ARE IMPORTANT IN CONFESSION AND FORGIVENESS

Years ago a famous movie was produced around the theme, "Love is never having to say you're sorry." There is an element of truth in the idea that genuine love may be required to go beyond the point of expressions of sorrow or confession of wrong. But there is also a sense in which the best kind of love *does* require words—words of affection, words of apology, and words of forgiveness.

There is only one relationship in which this balance of confession is one-sided, and that is the relationship we have with our Heavenly Father. We bring the confession of sin and He provides the response of forgiveness. We never use up our coupons at the throne of grace and we never have to worry that He gets tired of hearing our shabby list of sins, our unending list of needs. In fact, Hebrews 4:15-16 tells us:

> For we do not have a high priest who is unable to sympathize with our weaknesses, but we have One who has been tempted in every way, just as we are— yet was without sin. Let us then approach the throne of grace with confidence, so that we may receive mercy and find grace to help us in our time of need.

When dealing with another human being, the balance is different; in every relationship we are both sinner and sinned-against. Whether we are seeking forgiveness or giving it, we must face the fact that we are all in need of the grace of God. As Everett L. Worthington says:

> There are sins that are just between you and God. Those are forgiven and forgotten when they are confessed. But when we sin against God by sinning directly against someone else, it is like squeezing a toothpaste tube. Once the toothpaste is out on your hand, it's a mess. You can try to force it back into the tube, but it never all fits back. You can stick your hand in your pocket and try to cover up the sin, but

that just makes your own body messy. In James 5,
provision is made for the healing of social sins. That
calls for confession to others.[6]

Words provide closure. Confession lays out on the
table the bare truth of what we are and what we have
done. Forgiveness gathers up all the broken pieces of
our sin and inadequacy and carefully wraps them in
the sturdy fabric of love. Grace quietly puts them
away forever!

TWELVE

WHY GRIEVING
IS ESSENTIAL
TO FORGIVING

Life requires ceremonies. Not only cultures we call "civilized," but also in the remotest tribes, ceremonies govern all the rudimentary acts of living and dying. For some there are ceremonies that accompany seasons, planting and reaping, coming of age and marriage. For all, there are rites and rituals that mark birth and death.

Especially do we need ceremonies to mark our celebrations and our grieving. In fact, the grieving rituals are so important in some cultures that people are paid to mourn.

In our modern preoccupation with avoiding pain of any kind, we often try to bypass the grieving process. We falsely assume that minimizing the rituals of grief will somehow lessen the impact of our sorrow and loss.

My husband and I had been married less than a year when our first baby arrived seven weeks early, two days before Christmas. Besides the difficulties of his premature birth, that precious little boy was born without a lower jaw. He died within the hour.

We were shocked and devastated. "I don't understand," my sister said, voicing our own feelings. "Things like this don't happen in our family!"

"It will be easier for you," the doctor said, "if you don't give the baby a name and don't have a funeral. There is a place in the cemetery for preemies, called 'Babyland.' Let the funeral director take care of everything. Don't worry; you will have other children."

And so, in our numb compliance, we did whatever others told us to do. On Christmas morning, as my husband sat by my hospital bed, our firstborn was buried, nameless, in an unmarked grave.

Almost furtively, my dad and sister followed the hearse that carried that little body to the cemetery and standing in the snow, they sang together, "God's Way Is the Best Way." Then after reading a passage of Scripture and offering a simple prayer for Don and me, they turned and came home.

I was almost ashamed to talk about my loss. Everybody reminded me that I was healthy and young and we would have other beautiful, perfect children.

And we did. Eventually God gave us four children who have been the delight of our lives. But I discovered that grieving *has* to have expression. Every single December that followed, a great sadness hit me the week before Christmas. For years I attributed it to the pressures of the holidays. Finally, one day I realized that I was observing an annual process of grieving for that little one I had never seen and had never held in my arms.

After a while I learned to call him by his name, the one picked out before his birth. And even now, almost forty years later, when Christmas comes I take a few hours to celebrate and grieve the life of that child I will not see until I pass through heaven's gates.

I needed the ritual of grieving so many years ago, and would have been better off for it. The grieving process brings closure and release.

GRIEVING OUR LOSSES

Even when we recognize the need to grieve the loss of one claimed by death, we often fail to realize that the same kind of grieving process is necessary in any major loss:

marriage broken by divorce
loss of job
loss of home because of a major move
accident or loss of health
broken family relationships or friendships
loss of dreams or goals.

Several women whose marriages were either broken or damaged by marital infidelity on the part of their husbands wrote these impressions of the experience:

"I had periods of great self-pity when I felt no one could possibly understand my pain. I found that wallowing was easier than getting out of the mud."

"My failure to grieve was like a huge pile of unfinished business cluttering my life and heart. Until I faced each emotional transaction that was required, I couldn't file away the pain."

"I skipped the whole grieving process, or tried to, and hardly missed a beat in carrying my part of the responsibility—defending, forgiving, 'doing the right things,' being a good example, etc. In failing to admit my great pain and loss, I suffered great patches of depression and totally missed some of the confrontations . . . that would have brought quicker healing."

"I am realizing—very slowly and painfully—that many of my losses are as final as death and cannot be treated as a temporary discomfort."

"I do think that when I work through this, I will be more 'genuine.' Already I feel some relief in having been forced to give up some of my expectations. It is very hard when one keeps hoping that someday all the disappointment will magically go away."

"For me, grief has to be talked about, examined, thought about, felt, compared, measured by Scripture, explained, corrected, questioned, and given an outlet in some creative way. If I don't know what else to do, I do what I am doing today—simply writing, writing, writing, hoping somehow to flush out all the pain."

"What I am hoping is that I will be able, somehow and soon, to put what I am feeling in context of everything I know about God and the Bible."

"Grief is cleansing, but it is also exhausting. . . . The more intense it is, the more it must be measured into controllable doses."

"I always think I'm further along in the grieving process than I really am, because grief is not constant. It comes and goes with stimuli—pressure, remembrance, a chance remark."

Almost anyone going through heartache, whatever its source, can identify with some of these comments. More than anything else, we are made vividly conscious of the fact that grieving is a process. It requires attention and time to do its work.

It may be that the kind of grief that goes with divorce or a sense of betrayal in marriage requires a different kind of grace. In some ways, the grief that accompanies the loss of a mate or a child by death is a "clean" grief, like the pain which results from a surgeon's scalpel. The other may be described as "dirty" grief, like a wound from an accident—jagged with bruises and embedded dirt. When a person we love dies, there is a system of mourning that gives us closure and comfort. Friends surround us; cards and flowers give us an awareness that people understand and care for us. Even though we may struggle for a long time with one or more stages of the grieving process, the finality of death pulls us toward a final resolution.

But if a person is removed from our lives because of a divorce or some great sin which has been committed against us, we mourn as well the absence of a relationship that was once loving. We may have to mourn other losses as well, and often we have to mourn them alone. There are no sweet ceremonies to comfort us, no groups of friends surrounding us, no cards or flowers to help us through those first painful hours.

IDENTIFYING OUR LOSSES

1. Loss of trust. It is painful to acknowledge the loss of trust in the person who has hurt us. Frequently, a loss of confidence in the very one we should have been able to trust the most creates a lack of trust in other people. Whole categories of human beings—men, women, pastors, doctors, rich men or truck drivers!—are apt to be forever suspect, when we have lost our faith in one person.

It is true that trust may be regained, and this ought to be the goal in any damaged relationship, but trust is not something that can be restored by an act of the will.

Occasionally someone will advise that in order to forgive, trust must also be established. But trust is an element of experience and grows with the trustworthiness of the one who has broken faith. Forgiveness, though sometimes a process, begins with a choice to offer itself. Trust has to build its own road home.

That is not to say that the building of trust is a one-sided affair. One of the hardest steps in the healing process of forgiveness is the very act of facing the loss of confidence we feel when our faith in another person who is close to us has been destroyed. Yet it is essential that we name the loss to ourselves; and it surely must be addressed in any serious discussion with the one who has hurt us and wants restoration.

2. Loss of safety. When there is a breach of trust, there is often a loss of security as well. It may involve a loss of financial security as often happens through divorce; physical safety, as in the case of abuse; or simply a loss of confidence in the future and what it will bring.

The following lines, written by a woman going through the heartache resulting from her husband's infidelity, express this great loss of confidence in the future:

> *I am afraid of the normal casual exercise of daily living that covers some dark pit I can't see—the longings and lusts that have nothing to do with me, the traces of your life lived secretly and discovered randomly, that you cover with the words, "I forgot to tell you."*
>
> *I am afraid of this life we live together side by side, without touch, without hearing, without seeing—full of familiar polite conversation and even abstract discussions about our values, our needs and our pain—but always in the framework of "life"—not in the context of this lump that lies so heavy where confidence should be.*
>
> *I am afraid to forget; I am afraid to forgive lest I should live without caution—relax in the false comfort of hope and find the volcano exploding just at the moment I think I am finding my heart's ease—unsuspecting, unprotected, devastated.*

3. Loss of self-esteem. When we have been hurt by a broken relationship, we miss not only the catharsis of going through a public funeral and the rituals of death; we also lose a sense of our own self-worth. We somehow feel devalued by the things that have happened in our lives.

If the inability to grieve the great pain that goes with damaged relationships, particularly those ending in divorce, makes such a great impact in the lives of those who have been hurt (and all parties *are* hurt in a divorce!), it also affects their ability to forgive.

All forgiveness, for any offense that has hurt us, demands a certain amount of grieving. *We cannot fully forgive what we do not fully acknowledge as a significant loss.*

For this reason it is important that we not minimize our losses and the wrongs done against us. We should not say,

"Maybe it wasn't such a big deal. I shouldn't let it bother me so much."

"I don't like to talk about bad things."

"It just hurts worse if you talk about it."

"The faster I forget all about it, the sooner I can get on with my life."

"I'm a Christian so I have to learn to just put up with the things that hurt."

All of these statements slam the lid on all the resources God has provided for getting through pain and bringing about a kind of forgiveness that does not compromise personal integrity.

In the book *Love Is a Choice*, authors Hemfelt, Minirth and Meier say this:

> *The grief process is built into us, which is reason enough to suggest that it is the way God planned for us to deal with loss, emotional turmoil, and pain. When we abort that process, we end up forgiving (and no doubt quite sincerely) in an atmosphere of emotional dishonesty. Even though we voice forgiveness, there remains a deep reservoir of anger and resentment. The forgiveness lacks the integrity of reflecting all the facts of being human.*[1]

THE RESULTS OF FORGIVING WITHOUT GRIEVING

1. Self-pity. In the beginning, grief and self-pity can look very much alike. The difference between them is that while real grief eventually heals and lifts up, self-pity be-

comes a slow spiral into depression and despair.

Paul W. Powell writes, "Self-pity is easily the most destructive of the non-pharmaceutical narcotics; it is addictive, it gives momentary pleasure, and it separates the victim from reality."[2]

"When we validate our hurt and realize we don't have to deny the offense," says Dr. Gary Rosberg, "we are free to forgive. But this means looking inside and facing our pain. Our tendency is to pull away and deny it happened, hoping it will go away. . . . It's often painful to admit our hurts, but it's the first step to restoring relationships."[3]

2. Unacknowledged anger. If we refuse to look at the hurt we experience when someone has disappointed us, we are apt to feel anger, or perhaps even rage, without understanding why or against whom our anger is directed!

A recent survey indicated that more American women of all socioeconomic groups are injured by the abusive men in their lives than by rapes, muggings and automobile accidents combined! Sometimes alcohol becomes the poison that turns a loving husband into a vicious enemy. Often the catalyst for violence in abusive men is a lifetime of frustration and failure that has no outlet for expression except in the attacks they make on their own families.

Now a stranger phenomenon is appearing; women who have suffered a lifetime of abuse are resorting not merely to defending themselves, or to seeking help, but to the murder of their abusers!

If battered women knew what to do when they were abused, if they dared to call it violence, to grieve their losses and to access resources that would provide help, these horror stories could be prevented.

Unfortunately, many battered women do not know what to do with the pain of abuse; they either assume they are "bad people" who have somehow caused the violence, or they try to pretend it does not exist. Because the evil is never acknowledged, it is neither grieved nor corrected.

It is a frightening thing to feel so powerful an emotion as

rage without knowing exactly what it is or why we feel the way we do! Yet many people—perhaps more than we imagine—*are* consumed with anger that comes close to being uncontrollable. I suspect that many of those who go on shooting rampages in shopping malls, subway trains or restaurants are people who have never learned how to grieve their losses and to let go of them. There are always presenting causes, of course—loss of a job, a broken marriage, financial setback—but in themselves these hardly seem insurmountable enough for such dire reactions. It appears that a lifetime of buried grief and anger finally explodes into violence that cannot be controlled.

3. Depression. While depression may have many sources, both emotional and physiological, it is a common response to problems which seem unsolvable, or to situations over which we feel we have no control.

It would be foolish for those of us who are not professionals to attempt a quick or definitive judgment about the specific causes of depression in any individual who suffers its effects. Yet it is true that in many cases, learning how to grieve our losses, in context of a true biblical picture of God and ourselves, can make a difference in our ability to handle the disappointments of life.

Most of us love the Book of Psalms, and perhaps read it more often than any other book of the Bible. Nowhere in the Scripture is there more beautiful language, more exalted praise to the God of heaven! Sometimes we find a mixture of anguish because of trouble, prayers for deliverance, and then a concluding tribute of praise to God.

Psalm 88, however, is unique because it contains almost nothing of praise. It is almost entirely the pitiful cry of a man who is obviously in deep depression! Here are the closing lines of the psalm:

> From my youth I have been afflicted and close to death;
> I have suffered Your terrors and am in despair.

Your wrath has swept over me;
  Your terrors have destroyed me.
All day long they surround me like a flood;
  they have completely engulfed me.
You have taken my companions and loved ones from me;
  the darkness is my closest friend (Psalm 88:15-18).

Are you tempted to wonder why in the world God would choose to put such a depressing account in the Scriptures? Can it be because the pouring out of grief is part of the plan of God to bring resolution and eventual healing?

God is not shocked or horrified at the expressions of our grief, however depressing, however accusatory they seem to be; He already reads our hearts! And the acknowledging and identifying of the sources of our pain help to bring us to a point where we can let go and forgive.

A number of years ago Dr. Elizabeth Kubler-Ross outlined the steps of the grieving process which she discovered in terminally ill patients. These stages ran the gamut from shock and denial to eventual acceptance and resolution. In later studies by other psychologists, Dr. Kubler-Ross' steps in grieving were applied to other kinds of trauma and loss. Even though not everyone would agree that there is a predictable passage from shock to acceptance and resolution, those who go through losses can often afterward identify the various steps that were involved in their healing. When the loss involves the pain of moral failure or betrayal of one we have trusted, then one element of resolution must be forgiveness.

FORGIVENESS AS THE CONCLUSION OF GRIEVING

Can you imagine a world in which forgiveness is never practiced? We are always being offended and offending others. Life is so full of unfulfilled longings, unrequited love and disappointed dreams that we are always going to come into conflict with people we believe are blocking our happiness.

All too often we try to soothe the pain by food or by drugs; we rush around frantically filling our days with a relentless pursuit of duty or with senseless foolishness. And in the end we are consumed with bitterness at the people who failed to meet our needs and at God who allowed it all to happen.

How do we move from grieving to forgiving?

1. Begin by acknowledging the reality of what happened and the resulting pain.

"I always write a letter to the person who has hurt me," a friend told me the other day. "I write down my impression of what happened, and then I tell how it made me feel. At the end, I always encourage the other person to straighten me out on my facts, in case I haven't really understood what took place."

"Do you always mail it?" I asked.

"No, I wouldn't dare do that, at least not right away," she said, laughing. "I wouldn't have any friends left! I hold it for a couple of weeks, think about it, and pray about it. By that time I usually have a better perspective, or I'm done grieving or feeling hurt, and I just throw the letter away. If the problem is still bothering me, I sometimes take the letter to my pastor's wife to let her look at it and see what she thinks. If I do mail a letter, I usually feel confident that I am doing the right thing."

There is something very practical about writing down grievances when one is working through hurt. It helps one to clarify and define what happened and sometimes points out hurt feelings that have come from vague impressions or a misunderstanding of facts. It gives a verbal outlet for expressing anger and grief without hurting other people in the process. Last of all, it forces the writer to look over his own responses and to judge them more accurately after a little time has lapsed.

Since I am a rather visual person, I put nearly everything that is important to me in black and white, including various problems I am working on. When I write these out as a prayer to the Lord, even though He already knows what is going on in my heart, I have the added advantage of presenting my case to my Advocate who not only knows how I feel, but has the capacity to do something about the situation!

Eventually, many of the things we write down in the grieving process may need to be destroyed. This, in itself, can be a symbolic part of resolution and forgiveness. Whether that list of angry complaints against another is finally burned, shredded and flushed down the toilet, or simply discarded with the garbage, it allows the one who has been hurt to say, "I am done with this thing that has hurt me. I have chosen to forgive and put it away from my conscious memory. I will leave the conclusions with God."

> Grieving over wounds and taking responsibility may seem easy to some people. Like fixing an engine or solving a math problem, there are principles to help us accomplish what we're trying to do. But many of us don't even know where the engine is or what page the problem is on. And when we do finally get started, we generally have to unlearn skills which prevent problem-solving before we acquire new, needed skills.[4]

At the beginning of the grieving process, we are rarely able to deal with the pain alone. God has designed the body of Christ to provide the mutual support and comfort and admonition necessary to each one within the family as we face heartache and disappointment. Here are God's instructions:

> If you have any encouragement from being united with Christ, if any comfort from His love, if any fellowship with the Spirit, if any tenderness and compassion, then make my joy complete by being like-minded, having the same love, being one in spirit

and purpose. . . . Each of you should look not only to your own interests, but also to the interests of others" (Philippians 2:1-4).

Sometimes a Christian friend can help us through the grieving process, but many times we will require the help of a wise, godly pastor or a professional counselor. It does not indicate a lack of faith or limited spirituality to seek professional help. However, all counseling, whatever its source, should be measured by the truth of the Word of God.

2. Deal with anger in a biblical way. In Galatians 5:20, the Apostle Paul lists among the acts of the sinful nature, "hatred, discord, jealousy, fits of rage, selfish ambition, dissensions, factions and envy." Any of these may be the source or the conclusion of anger. Because the origin of our anger is not always clear, we need to be honest in examining it by the Word of God and in searching our own hearts, so that we will know for sure where it comes from.

Sometimes anger is the natural reaction to a specific evil act committed against us. In Ephesians 4:26-27 Paul warns, "In your anger do not sin. Do not let the sun go down while you are still angry, and do not give the devil a foothold."

How can we avoid letting "the sun go down" on our anger, when there are still steps to be taken in the grieving process? What if the sinner has not yet been confronted? What if no resolution has occurred? The answer, it seems to me, is to be found in the following verses:

Do not let any unwholesome talk come out of your mouths, but only what is helpful for building others up according to their needs, that it may benefit those who listen. And do not grieve the Holy Spirit of God, with whom you were sealed for the day of redemption" (Ephesians 4:29-30).

We do not sin in "feeling" anger; we sin when we allow it to either fester inside or to erupt in behavior or words that hurt others and grieve the Holy Spirit. Every day that anger occurs, God wants us to make sure that we deposit it with Him before we go to bed. Perhaps we have not done with it all we will have to do, and perhaps forgiveness is not yet complete, but we have determined we will not let it destroy us or other people.

3. Identify the symptoms of depression. While depression may come and go and have varying stages of intensity in any person's life, there are certain clues that nearly always identify a need to get help.

In his book *Crisis Counseling*, H. Norman Wright lists eleven common symptoms of depression:

A feeling of hopelessness, despair, sadness and apathy
A loss of perspective and negative thinking patterns
Changes in eating and sleeping patterns
A general loss of self-esteem
Withdrawal from others
A desire to escape from problems or from life itself
Irritability and frequent crying
An inability to concentrate or make decisions
Misdirected anger
A sense of guilt, real or imagined
A sense of helplessness, dependence on others.[5]

Don't simply try to "wait out" a depression. Get whatever help is available, including medical help, if necessary.

If you are in the depression phase of grieving, you may need to remind yourself often, "This too shall pass." But don't assume that simply talking yourself out of pain will work. Get help!

As much as is possible, keep up your normal routines. Getting dressed and going to work even when you don't feel like it will be better than sitting at home brooding.

Exercise is known to be of special benefit for those suffering from depression. There is both emotional and physical restoration that comes with vigorous activity; get involved in whatever brought you pleasure before you were depressed.

It is possible that the most difficult time of day will be morning, after a sleepless night. Don't allow yourself to lie in bed with your mind running down all the dark alleys of gloom. Choose to look for small pleasures in the sights and sounds around you. Remind yourself that you are one day closer to healing.

In my own bout with depression several years ago, I discovered that I could control how I felt for about five minutes at a time. If I deliberately pulled my mind out of the morbid thoughts that came so readily, and listed (out loud) everything I could think of that was good and beautiful, I could hold off the shadows in my mind for at least a little while longer.

While I did not particularly appreciate other people casually throwing Bible verses at me to "cheer me up," I did have one or two verses which I felt the Lord had given to me personally for that particular time in my life, and they were a great comfort to me.

4. Work on the perfectionism that requires a flawless world. A great deal of our grieving is ultimately related to the fact that we refuse to give up our expectations of how life is supposed to be! If we find that we are constantly upset with things that do not work as they should, with people who are unreliable or undisciplined, with plans that have to be changed or delayed, or with our own inadequacies, then we will have to face the fact that we are refusing to let God be God! We do, indeed, live in a flawed world; but God's will in our lives is not frustrated by those things and people who have been damaged by sin.

Second Corinthians 1:3-4 says, "Praise be to the God and Father of our Lord Jesus Christ, the Father of compassion and the God of all comfort, who comforts us in all our troubles, so that we can comfort those in any trouble with the comfort we ourselves have received from God." Dealing with our own frustrations equips us with the tools to encourage others in their struggle with perfectionism!

5. Accept the fact that forgiveness may not be accompanied with a warm feeling that all is right with the world. Many things in life have to be done, not because they are comfortable or easily accomplished, but simply because they are right. When we make our choices on the basis of conviction instead of comfort, God will give the grace until the feelings come.

THIRTEEN

THE HOME: GOD'S GRADUATE COURSE IN FORGIVENESS

W hat's an ideal home supposed to be like, anyway? Is it a place where children play quietly, rooms stay clean, the telephone never rings at the wrong moment, and dinner always gets to the table on time for a waiting, cheerful family?

Probably not. But sometimes our expectations *are* this unrealistic!

A man picturing the ideal home would probably not include Saturday morning chores, a wife's lengthy recital of the day's activities, children with runny noses, or a meal prepared to limit fat grams! It might include Little League baseball games but probably not piano recitals. It might include a budget that allows for hockey game tickets but probably not boudoir chairs.

What kind of wife fits into the ideal home, according to most men? That one is easy. The ideal wife is the very woman he assumed his wife to be when he married her! One cynic wrote, "A man marries a woman hoping she will not change; a woman marries a man, hoping she will be able to change him!" Let's hope neither of those is entirely true!

What would a woman consider the ideal home? One where meals are eaten by candlelight? After-dinner clean-up is a shared experience? Faucets don't leak and babies sleep through the night?

CINDERELLA AND PRINCE CHARMING

Even in our age when many women feel they are capable of making it on their own, I suspect that a typical woman still carries in the back of her mind a kind of Cinderella dream. She hopes that somewhere, sometime, a Prince Charming will rescue her from her chimney corner (or office desk), and carry her off on a white horse to the castle, where she will live happily ever after!

But it is possible that Prince Charming will turn out to be a couch potato, barely coming up for air between the Superbowl, the NBA Playoffs and the World Series.

It is possible that Prince Charming snores, picks his teeth, and leaves his socks on the floor. Or that he inevitably forgets to call when he works late and hates to mow the lawn.

On the other hand, Cinderella may not fit very well into the fairy tale either.

Perhaps she cries over nothing at all, talks too much, and hasn't the slightest idea how to balance a checkbook. It's altogether possible that the size eight wedding dress will never again fit.

Seen up close in the fairly intimate contacts of marriage, most of us discover that Prince Charming's armor is a little more rusty than we had noticed. And Cinderella's golden slippers are beginning to look a little run-down at the heels!

But what if Prince Charming's failures turn out to be the kinds of problems you thought happened only to other people?

What if he can't keep a good job?

What if he has an affair?

What if he turns out to be abusive?

On the other hand:

What if Cinderella turns bitter and hateful?
What if she has an emotional breakdown?
What if she becomes seriously ill?

Pretty quickly we discover that marriage has a lot more to do with automobile repairs than it does with white horses; it includes a lot more drudgery than dancing! As Stephen Brown says, "If you live in a fallen world, you are going to have to live with the implications of a fallen world."[1]

Life is not a fairy tale, not a romantic novel or the substance of a love song. All the romantic elements we can add to it are important, but marriage requires more.

> *Marriage has been called man's most difficult, if not impossible, enterprise. The demands we make upon it, the expectations we have for it, the rewards we hope to get from it—these are enormous. . . . In the long run, though, it seems that Abraham Lincoln, of all people, had the commonsense answer to what people want and get from their marriages. "Most folks," he said, "are as happy as they make up their minds to be."[2]*

There are three common fallacies about marriage:

"Marriage is supposed to make me happy."
"If I marry a Christian, everything will turn out right!"
"If I just love my mate enough, he/she will meet all my needs!"

What we forget is that marriage is made up of two people who have agendas of their own, two people who are limited by their own backgrounds and perceptions and personalities, and who struggle daily with an innate desire to meet their own needs first of all. Even when they truly love each other and are committed to pleasing God, their daily choices and their basic attitudes are colored by a nature flawed with sin.

THREE BIBLICAL FACTS ABOUT MARRIAGE

1. Marriage is supposed to be a ministering relationship to both husband and wife, to the children who are added to the family, and then to the church and community. Ecclesiastes 4:9-12 says:

> *Two are better than one,*
> *because they have a good return for their work:*
> *If one falls down, his friend can help him up.*
> *But pity the man who falls*
> *and has no one to help him up!*
> *Also, if two lie down together, they will keep warm.*
> *But how can one keep warm alone?*
> *Though one may be overpowered, two can defend*
> *themselves.*
> *A cord of three strands is not quickly broken.*

The traditional marriage vows include a number of spiritual and emotional gifts which the partners promise to each other, including "to love, honor, and cherish 'til death do us part." And whether or not they are included in the wedding vows, the Word of God includes other things we "owe" to one another. See 1 Peter 3:1-7; Ephesians 5:28-31; Genesis 2:24; 1 Corinthians 7:3-5; Colossians 3:18-19, for instance.

Remarkable for its absence is the promise, "I guarantee to make you happy for the rest of your life!" Why is it not included? Because no human being has the capacity to make another human being happy. That is something that must come from inside ourselves as a by-product of our commitment to God and our love for other people. *Marriage was not designed simply to make us happy!*

> *It is impossible to eliminate expectations. Even if it*
> *were possible, it would not be desirable. Expecta-*
> *tions are the fizz in the soda pop of life. What so*

frequently happens, however, is that we create unrealistic *expectations. We look especially to those we
love to meet our needs, build our egos, and affirm us
in what we do. When they fail to do this to our satisfaction, we are crushed.*[3]

2. Marriage is designed to be a living, growing organism. Remember how eagerly you watched for every little evidence of growth and change in your first
baby?

You were delighted with the first nebulous smile,
the first precariously balanced attempt to sit up, the
first wobbly step, the first drink from a cup, the first
day of an undiapered bottom.

Later, after you had guided that same precious
child through measles, piano lessons, basketball
practices, and the first driver's license, you looked
back with wistfulness to the closeness and interdependence of those early experiences. Perhaps you
thought, with a sigh, of how wonderful those days
were, and wished it were possible to turn the clock
back to those days of babyhood.

But a living organism is designed by God to grow
and change, and we would be alarmed if that pliant
little body of the baby—so frequently cuddled and
admired—did not change. We would be exhausted if
that three-month-old baby needed us exactly the
same way for the rest of his life.

Marriage is a living, growing organism too. Just as
a new baby grows and changes, so marriage must
change. The essence of romantic poetry and music
and novels is an expression of love in its flowering,
infant stage—the mystique of two hearts irresistably
drawn together, the fascination with another's mind
and interests and dreams, the admiration of another
human body, so different from one's own. There is
an interdependence in the beginning stages of love

that is so intense a lover feels incomplete (and perhaps even desolate) without the presence of the beloved other half.

For a while, lovers are obsessed with "firsts" and are delighted with new experiences involved in the bonding of two lives in marriage—the first home, the first company meal, perhaps even the first quarrel! They live on the magic of discovery. Every mundane thing in life takes on significance, because it is enhanced by the newness of experiences as a duet instead of a solo!

While the intensity of bonding with another human being is exhilarating and enriching, it is also exhausting. Eventually, in every relationship, there must come times of aloneness and separateness, time to refill one's own emotional tank, time to recognize one's own value entirely apart from the connections of marriage or parenthood or to society as a whole.

Sometimes, in those early days of bonding in marriage, one partner begins to demand, either verbally or by emotional manipulation, a total absorption into the life of the other partner. There is a frantic attempt to be involved with every activity, every thought, every dream. Any retreat into one's own heart, any move toward outside friendships, any pursuit of personal goals, is viewed as conspiracy against the relationship.

The more pressure applied—even the pressure of overwhelming attention and intense adoration—the greater the need to close doors in the mind and heart, to find privacy and autonomy.

A good marriage is not an organism in which individual characteristics are so absorbed and blended that there is no sense of personal identity. If there are not contrasting viewpoints, the weights and counterweights of personality differences, strengths and weaknesses of male and female responses, the contrasting influences of early environment, the result will be a narrowness of viewpoint and a limited capacity to understand others. In a good relationship, "iron sharpens iron."

Shift, if you can, to another picture, of marriage as a sophisticated piece of machinery. Just as the moving gears of a machine mesh with other gears and thereby produce energy or commodities, so two partners in a marriage mesh together in a continuing pattern—constantly coming together and then moving apart, each working together at their point of contact, but differing even as gears may differ in size and speed and material, yet still moving together for common goals.

The oil which keeps the gears running smoothly is, of course, love. "Love is patient, love is kind," says 1 Corinthians 13. "It does not envy, it does not boast, it is not proud. It is not rude, it is not self-seeking, it is not easily angered, it keeps no record of wrongs. Love does not delight in evil but rejoices with the truth. It always protects, always trusts, always hopes, always perseveres."

It is interesting to note that verse 11 of that same chapter says, "When I was a child, I talked like a child, I thought like a child, I reasoned like a child. When I became a man, I put childish ways behind me."

There is a sense in which any relationship, and particularly marriage, produces a greater capacity to forgive. Childish selfishness and childish tantrums are relinquished in the desire to meet the needs of the beloved.

3. Marriage does not insulate us from pain or loneliness or disappointment. The Word of God, which gives us an accurate picture of life and society in all generations, abounds with illustrations of marriages requiring great forgiveness.

There is Leah, unloved and bitter, and there is her husband, Jacob, a man who thought he was marrying the beautiful Rachel but was tricked by her desperate father into marrying the older sister first. Leah reflects a wistfulness in her choice of names for her first two sons. "She named (the first) Reuben, for she said, 'It is because the Lord has seen my misery. Surely my husband will love me now.' She conceived again, and when she gave birth to a son she said, 'Because the Lord heard that I am not loved, He gave me this one too.' So she named him Simeon" (Genesis 29:32-33). Eventually Leah has more sons and at the birth of the fourth one, she is able to say, "This time I will praise the Lord."

We could look at Leah's heartache and use it as a good illustration that life simply is not fair! In fact, when we look at the entire lifestyle of Jacob, his father-in-law, Laban, his two wives, Rachel and Leah, and his twelve sons, we see jealousy, intrigue, lying, pain, and disappointment. Why does God choose to air all that dirty laundry? And more important, how could such a dysfunctional family contribute anything significant to God's plan for His people?

What we have to remember is that all the tools God uses to do His work, whether we are talking about individuals or families or organizations, are flawed. "We have this treasure in earthen vessels," the Apostle Paul says. We are all "little cracked pots"; still, God chooses to work His plan through us. And so God used Leah and Jacob and their murderous sons. Eventually Jacob had a personal encounter with God and he was never the same again. Leah's fourth child, Judah, became the head of the kingly line through whom the Messiah would come. Leah was not the favorite wife, but she was the one whose body lay in the cave-tomb of the husband whose love she sought all her life. Her sister and rival, Rachel, died in childbirth while traveling and could not be buried in the family tomb.

God does not promise that any of us will have the perfect marriage. All of our relationships are marked by our own failure, by the circumstances God allows in our lives, and by the wickedness of the world around us. What He does promise is that He will be with us in the pain and will give us the power to live triumphantly, even when we may not understand His purposes. Hebrews 10:35-36 says, "So do not throw away your confidence; it will be richly rewarded. You need to persevere so that when you have done the will of God, you will receive what He has promised."

Marriage is a learning experience. We learn how to balance our own needs and our own weaknesses with the needs and frailties of that one with whom we have chosen to spend a lifetime.

If we do our homework well, we will discover that all of the things we thought we needed for happiness will come, not through the demands we make of others, but in the gentle relinquishing of our rights for the sake of the other as we learn, "It is more blessed to give than to receive."

CHILDREN

God has designed children to be an extension of the ministry of marriage, a source of personal growth and blessing, an opportunity to invest in the future.

In an age when we see children abused or neglected, children who murder their parents, children who are aborted for convenience' sake, and children who become third-generation recipients of welfare, young couples are sometimes tempted to opt out of parenthood. Even in Christian circles we rarely hear people quote the blessing of children as given in Psalm 127:3-5:

> *Lo, children are an heritage of the Lord; and the*
> *fruit of the womb is His reward. As arrows are in the*
> *hand of a mighty man, so are children of one's youth.*
> *Happy is the man who hath his quiver full of them;*
> *they shall not be ashamed, but they shall speak with*
> *the enemies in the gate (KJV).*

Why are children often valued so little these days? A number of years ago, advice columnist Ann Landers conducted an informal survey, asking her readers the question, "If you could start all over again, would you have children?"

The results of the poll shocked Ann Landers, and perhaps many of her readers as well. The overwhelming evidence was that most people, given the chance to start over, would not have children. It was not necessarily the parents of young children—those who were having to invest the greatest amount of time in parenting—who complained. It was the parents of teenagers who were frustrated with their inability to control "bad" behavior, and the parents of adult children whose offspring were ungrateful and unloving.

Can it be that most parents have expectations for their children which are impossible to fulfill? When their expectations are disappointed, they harbor bitterness and frustration, feeling that somehow parenthood cheated them out of what they thought they had a right to expect.

What should we expect of our children? What are children *for*?

1. Children *should* provide immediate and lifetime enjoyment—they should be just plain fun! Would anyone willingly take on the eternal responsibility for another human being if there were no pleasure, no satisfaction attached to the project?

Having said that, we have to clarify what kind of

pleasure we have a right to expect. A baby is not a doll to be dressed and played with when convenient; a little child is not a tiny performing robot manipulated to make his parents look good; a teenager is not an alter-ego to fulfill all his parents' lost dreams!

Children must be enjoyed for who they are, for their own unique attributes, for the mysterious blossoming of the individuals they are becoming, bearing the traces of parents, ancestors, and themselves.

Obviously, the joy of parenting is mixed with a sense of the awesomeness—and sometimes the awfulness—of the job! When children are not trained and disciplined, they bring great grief to their parents!

The Old Testament priest Eli is a powerful example of a good man who failed to give enough attention to the rearing of his children. The Scripture says of them, "Eli's sons were wicked men; they had no regard for the Lord" (1 Samuel 2:12). God laid the blame at the feet of Eli himself:

> See, I am about to do something in Israel that will make the ears of everyone who hears of it tingle. At that time I will carry out against Eli everything I spoke against his family—from beginning to end. For I told him that I would judge his family forever because of the sin he knew about; his sons made themselves contemptible, and he failed to restrain them (1 Samuel 3:11-13).

What anguish and heartache comes when parents fail to work at the hard job of parenting!

2. Children contribute to the personal growth and development of their own parents. Kevin Huggins says:

> I recently heard one newly married couple comment, "Marriage just doesn't work. Since we came home

*from the honeymoon all we do is talk about each
other's faults. It's as if marriage has brought out all
the worst things in each of us."*

*I thought to myself, "Their marriage is working for
them exactly as it's supposed to. It's bringing out the
worst things in each of them so that they can be dealt
with." That is what parent-child relationships are
supposed to do as well.*[4]

Joyce had just caught her little daughter Linda in
another major lie and she was terrified at the possibility of Linda becoming a chronic liar. She had tried
various kinds of punishment, quoted Scripture, and
given numerous lectures. Nothing was working.

In frustration, Joyce finally burst into tears. "The
reason I am so disturbed about this problem, Linda," she said through her tears, "is that I see myself
in you. All my life I have struggled with the problem
of being absolutely truthful, and you can't imagine
how much pain it has brought me. Now I can see that
I am going to have to get my problem fixed just as
you have to get yours fixed. I refuse to let you grow
up with this unfinished business. We are *both* going
to stick with this problem until it is resolved!"

Perhaps we have trouble forgiving our children for
their failures because we have not taken care of the
mirror-image of their faults in our own lives.

3. Children are designed by God to add a positive
contribution to society through the home, the community, the school, and the church. Our sphere of
influence is multiplied, for good or evil, when we
have children.

As I waited in the dentist's office one day, I met a
university professor, a sociologist who was also waiting for her appointment. When the conversation
came around to the state of the world as it is today,
the sociologist said, "Well, obviously things are going

to get worse and worse. That's the reason my husband and I decided we would never have children!"

She was right about one thing; the world is obviously getting worse and worse. And my heart skipped a beat as I thought of my own four who were about to enter that dangerous world!

Then suddenly I thought, "No! Our choice to have children was the right choice! Our kids can make a difference in the world. They can be that 'light on the hill' that shines out over a dark world; they can be the 'salt' that cleanses and heals a society sick with sin. And whatever investment my husband and I make in our children can extend beyond our own lifetime; they can make a difference in this generation and they can go beyond to generations who will never remember who we were!"

What God requires of me is that I provide the tools, the example, the encouragement. I do not get to choose the *how* or the *where* or even the *what*. If I acknowledge that my children are simply on loan to be enjoyed for a time and trained for eternity, then I will not be bitter and frustrated at what God chooses to do with their lives.

If I require my children to follow my agenda, to meet my needs, then even my training and discipline will be hampered by my personal dreams; if I encourage them to seek God's will for their lives, then I can leave the choices and the enabling in the hands of God.

As Kevin Huggins writes:

> It is always a mark of an unhealthy parent-teen relationship when parents look to their adolescents to help meet the crucial desires only God can fulfill. Parents who come to depend on their kids for this level of satisfaction end up fearing their own children far more than they fear God.[5]

4. What do our children have a right to expect from us?

They have a right to expect us to be consistent, to be fair, to be understanding—examples of redeemed sinners experiencing the grace of God.

They have a right to expect us to allow freedom for growth, for developing judgment, and for adventure, while providing walls that will keep them physically and spiritually safe. No little task!

They have a right to expect unconditional love and acceptance; not ignoring problems but loving beyond the problems.

They have a right to expect a foundation of forgiveness—assurance that no offense is beyond healing and restoration.

They have a right to expect absolute unyielding in moral issues, thoughtful discussion in social issues, and grace in matters of expediency.

They have a right to expect patience in the process!

FOURTEEN

HOW TO GET EVEN: DESIGN YOUR OWN "HIT LIST"

F
ifty-five pounds of dynamite and fifty blasting caps: that was the tool of vengeance Michael Stevens used to kill three members of his estranged wife's family and two other people who happened to be nearby, when the homemade bombs he had mailed to various family members went off.

While the police in the upstate New York communities where the six bombs were mailed were still sorting out the details of the Christmas week tragedy, investigators theorized that the bombs may have been designed to silence Michael Stevens' critics in his wife's family.

We are horrified at such a concept of justice. How could anyone plan so sinister a plot for any wrongdoing, deserved or undeserved?

But there is something in all of us that *does* want to see justice done, when we or someone we love has been hurt. A lot of us would easily identify with David's prayer in Psalm 94:1-2, "O Lord, the God who avenges, O God who avenges, shine forth. Rise up, O Judge of the earth; pay back to the proud what they deserve."

When people break the rules we want to see sin punished; we want justice done, and done immediately, particularly if the wrong has been done against us!

Unfortunately, our motives in seeking vengeance are of-

ten not so noble as David's probably were. Most of the
time, when I desire "justice," it is not for the glory of God
but for personal vindication. Knowing my own limited perspective, I am grateful that we have a God who is both
patient and compassionate without sacrificing His greater
justice to the pettiness of "getting even."

How should a child of God respond when he has been
treated unfairly, perhaps misunderstood or talked about,
or worse, deliberately hurt by the maliciousness of someone else?

One Christian writer has suggested that we ought to
have a "hit list"—not the kind the mafia uses for those
they will "wipe out," but a list of people we are committed
to loving and praying for, people who hurt us or who
make life difficult for us. Instead of praying for vengeance,
we should pray for healing and restoration and the blessing of God!

There are several beautiful examples of this type of response in the Word of God, of individuals who were able
to demonstrate their ability to pray for those who had hurt
them, and thereby to turn bitterness into blessing.

Take, for example, the criticism of Moses by Aaron and
Miriam. With the "bad press" Moses was always getting
from other people, he should have been able to count on
the support of his own sister and brother, but they were
obviously struggling with jealousy over Moses' position as
leader of the people of Israel. "Miriam and Aaron began to
talk against Moses because of his Cushite wife, for he had
married a Cushite. 'Has the Lord spoken only through
Moses?' they asked. 'Hasn't He also spoken through us?' "
(Numbers 12:1-2)

Notice how issues become confused when jealousy de-
velops. Aaron was a priest and God *had* spoken through
him; Miriam was a prophetess who had led the entire
population of women in a great song of praise after God's
rescue of Israel at the Red Sea. But now Moses' influence
was increasing; theirs was not. They couldn't fault Moses'

leadership, but they certainly could criticize his wife, and
that is exactly what they did!

If you have read the rest of the story, you know that God
came to Moses' defense and confirmed his special place by
pronouncing, "With him I speak face to face, clearly and
not in riddles; he sees the form of the Lord. Why then
were you not afraid to speak against My servant Moses?"
(v. 8)

God's anger was so aroused against these two that he
touched Miriam's body with leprosy and she was not
healed *until Moses prayed for her!* Moses' vindication was
in the fact that only *his* prayers could reverse the punishment of God upon his adversaries!

Then, there is Job. Sick, bereaved, destitute, stripped of
honor, he should have been able to expect genuine conso-
lation from his friends. Instead, what he got was lengthy
platitudes and unfair accusations.

Again God flew to the defense of this great man. He said
to the self-righteous friends of Job, "I am angry with you
and your two friends, because you have not spoken of Me
what is right, as My servant Job has. . . . My servant Job
will pray for you, and I will accept his prayer and not deal
with you according to your folly" (Job 42:7-8). The story
concludes with this interesting statement in Job 42:10,
"After Job had prayed for his friends, the Lord made him
prosperous again and gave him twice as much as he had
before."

What a vindication!

Finally, there is Stephen, that amazing New Testament
deacon who preached with such power and conviction
that his ungodly hearers "gnashed their teeth at him," and
stoned him in great fury. But even in the final moments of
such a death, Stephen was able to pray for those responsible, "Lord, do not hold this sin against them" (Acts 7:60).

From heaven, Stephen must have rejoiced to see his
final "vengeance" upon those who hated him, in the conversion of Saul whose testimony would change the world!

There is a right way to "get even" with those who have hurt you! You can *pray* for them—not that God will destroy them, but that He will use you to do His good work in their lives and bring glory to Himself.

Do you dare seek for that kind of vengeance? Do you dare *not* to?

The most sobering of all the prayers prayed by the innocent for the perpetrator of evil is Christ's prayer as He hung on the cross, dying for the sins of all mankind. He had been insulted, lied about, beaten, ridiculed, tortured, and now was dying in the most painful, humiliating way it was possible to die. And even while the people stood watching and sneering, He prayed, "Father, forgive them, for they do not know what they are doing" (Luke 23:34).

If there is any quality in the world that should mark the difference between the one who knows God personally, and the one who does not, it certainly should be this capacity to pray for those who have intended to do them harm.

PRAYING FOR THOSE WHO HAVE HURT US

1. In praying for people who have done wrong against us, we begin to clarify what the issues really are. Our efforts to differentiate between good intentions and bad intentions, between blame and innocence are, at best, flawed.

Just spend an hour or two in an average courtroom and you will understand what I mean. The prosecution will present an argument that sounds absolutely convincing—the man is guilty. But soon the defense will begin to present witnesses with "proof" that is totally contrary to what you have heard. Suddenly, the certainty begins to fade. Things are not, after all, quite as they seemed to be.

Perhaps you have stood on a street corner when a major accident occurred right before your eyes. The police came and questions were asked. You were confident of your answers; after all, you were standing right there when the accident happened! But there are other witnesses, other stories by "eye witnesses," and strange as it seems, the stories do not match!

When we pray for the one who has hurt us, we make it possible for the Lord to "explain" the issues to us, to clarify our own vision, and to purify our responses.

2. Praying for those who have done evil toward us gives us a chance to represent God before an ungodly world. In Luke 6:27-28, Jesus commanded, "Love your enemies, do good to those who hate you, bless those who curse you, pray for those who mistreat you." Why? "Because," Jesus said, "your reward will be great, and you will be the sons of the Most High, because He is kind to the ungrateful and wicked" (v. 35).

Janie is one of the busiest women I know. After rearing a large family successfully, she invests her time and energies in more ministries than I could count! Friends and strangers use her varied resources in many areas. On a given day she is likely to have helped to arrange a home loan for retired missionaries, worked with the family of a pregnant teenager, and set up a family seminar on a military base two hundred miles away. If there is any one thing Janie does not have much of, it is time! Of course, her friends know this, and they are happy to work with her schedule in order to spend time with her.

But Janie has a friend, an elderly Jewish lady who is bitter about the way life has treated her and her people. When she is lonely or angry or scared and needs a friend, she wants Janie, and she wants her immediately! Janie always finds a way to fit this angry old lady into her life, and when she prays for her, she prays for "my dear friend Rachel."

I am sure the relationship holds limited personal satisfaction for Janie. When she takes Rachel to lunch, most of the time is spent with Rachel's impatient questions, "Where were you last week when I called?" "Why do those

Baptists insist on parking in front of my house?" "If Jesus was the Messiah, why didn't He make the world a better place?"

What makes it possible for Janie to smile when she talks about "my friend, Rachel"? "I pray for her," Janie explains, "and I know that one of these days she is going to accept Jesus Christ as her personal Savior. I'm the only Christian she knows well, so I want to make sure I act like Jesus Christ would act."

Prayer is the power source that makes such a response possible.

3. Praying for our enemies is a way to produce reward in heaven. It is only when we have learned to pray for those who hate us because of our relationship with Jesus Christ that we can genuinely rejoice at the opportunity to suffer for Jesus' sake. When we retaliate against someone who has done wrong, we may feel justified in responding as we have, but that makes the conflict a "human" one instead of a "heavenly" one. If we can say instead, "Lord, I refuse to get even or to insist that I am right. Bless this person who delights in insulting me because of You. Fill the deepest needs of his heart," then we can identify with the fellowship of Christ's sufferings. Jesus said to His disciples, and to us, "Blessed are you when people insult you, persecute you, and falsely say all kinds of evil against you because of Me. Rejoice and be glad, because great is your reward in heaven" (Matthew 5:11-12).

4. Praying for our enemies is a way to find peace of heart, rest of mind. Have you ever been angry enough to feel the effects of that anger in your own body? Your heart races; you can feel your blood pressure rising, pounding in your head. Your face flushes and a knot tightens up in your stomach.

"I began to realize how dangerous anger could be," a friend told me, "when I stopped to identify what it was doing to me physically. Even when that first wave of sudden anger had subsided, I found that I was trembling because of all the adrenaline I had used!"

Imagine what happens when the issues that created that anger are never resolved. We may not be able to identify what is going on inside our bodies, but the effects take their toll. Whatever we are able to work out in relationships to bring physical relaxation and inner peace, we certainly ought to do. But in the end, for both the solvable and the unsolvable problems with people, we need to pray for them. That is what will bring rest of heart.

In Philippinans 4:6-7 we read, "Do not be anxious about anything, but in everything, by prayer and petition, with thanksgiving, present your requests to God. And the peace of God, which transcends all understanding, will guard your hearts and your minds in Christ Jesus."

That word "petition" has the same meaning as the old word, "supplication," which implies an earnestness in praying that few of us actually practice.

In his book, *God's Cure for Anxious Care*, John R. Rice says:

> *Why plead and beg and wait before God? Does He not already know our need? Is His heart so hard that we must beg Him to be compassionate and arouse His pity by our need? I am sure that is not the reason. The tender heart of God is ready now to give us everything we need.* But we ourselves are not ready! *The willfullness, the covetousness, the sin you committed but did not confess, the sin you yourself did not even see, the sin you love and hold on to, the sin that dishonors God—God must deal with your sin while you wait and pray. Perhaps your will must be changed to His will. Perhaps your prayer must be modified to honor His great name. Perhaps your motive is wrong even if your prayer is right. But the fires of supplication will melt away the dross in your prayer life and God will be able to give you what you need if you wait before Him. "Supplication" is part of*

*God's remedy for anxious care. Do not leave it out;
pray through.*[1]

BUILDING A MINISTRY OF PRAYER

1. Establish a pattern of prayer that will be easy to
continue on a daily basis.

There is something to be said for having a special
"place of prayer."

When I was a junior high school student, my men-
tor and model was a college senior who happened to
be a student teacher in the school I attended. She
sometimes invited me to go with her to various college functions—basketball games, music recitals, etc.
But when the college had "spiritual emphasis week,"
she told me gently that she would be sitting alone.

"I came to this school as a rebellious, angry fresh-
man," she said, "and one day when I was sitting in a
particular seat in the back of the chapel balcony,
God met me there and changed my life. Now when I
really want God to touch my life in a particular way, I
sit in that very same seat so that the Lord will know I
am expecting to meet Him there."

That isn't such a strange idea. When the Old Testament patriarch Jacob got into trouble and really
needed God to work in his life, he went back to
Bethel, that place where God first met him and
changed his life.

Whether or not your "Bethel" is a literal, physical
place, you need to know that there is a special secret
place where God will find you waiting. God is anywhere one who loves Him happens to be! He is, as
the poet Tennyson said, "nearer than breathing."
The precious Spirit of God makes His home within
our hearts, and we can speak to Him anytime we
want to do so! When the Lord Jesus was getting
ready for the cross, He promised, "I will ask the Fa-

ther, and He will give you another Counselor to be with you forever—the Spirit of truth. The world cannot accept Him, because it neither sees Him nor knows Him. But you know Him, for He lives with you and will be in you" (John 14:16-17). We need never be concerned that the Spirit is busy somewhere else!

When my children were small, much of my praying had to be done "on the run." Vacuuming was a good time for praying because I could pray (or cry) aloud if I wanted to, without others hearing. A lot of my praying in those days was done as I drove many miles chauffeuring children here and there. I also found that if I carried my prayer list with me on small cards, I could pray silently when I waited in doctors' or dentists' offices.

The point is that we must build habits of prayer.

2. Learn to be specific in your praying. It is not enough to pray, "Lord, bless so-and-so." Especially when we are praying for someone who is difficult to love, we need to make sure we know what it is we wish God to do. Our prayers may need to include:

"Lord, solve whatever the problem is in this person's life that makes him difficult to live with."

"Help this person to begin to understand how much his words hurt."

"Teach me to say the right things to this person so that I can sweeten the relationship."

"In some special way, Lord, reveal Yourself to this person today, so that he will long for Your presence in his life."

You will notice that very often our prayers for other people, especially difficult people, may have to include prayers for ourselves as we have contact with them.

3. Keep a prayer list. You may find that keeping a prayer journal in which you write your requests is helpful. Some find that putting the list of requests on

a sheet which is posted on the refrigerator, taped to a desk, or even mounted on the bathroom mirror helps them to remember to pray. I find that making out a 3 x 5 card for specific people for whom I pray on a daily basis encourages me to keep track of needs I am asking for and also of the very dates I take time to pray. Sometimes, at the end of the year I will mail the card to the one for whom I've prayed, saying, "I just wanted you to know that you were thought of and prayed for this past year." (Not a good idea if the prayer card records, "Lord, help Joe fix his rotten attitude!")

4. Tie your prayers to the Word of God. It is our involvement in the Scriptures that teaches us *how* to pray. James 4:2-3 says, "You do not have, because you do not ask God. When you ask, you do not receive, because you ask with wrong motives."

How can *any* of us know how to pray with the right motives, if we do not pray in relationship to what God tells us in His Word?

I suspect that all too often we think of prayer as a kind of superstitious ritual—like having a fairy godmother who rather arbitrarily waves a magic wand to grant us our three wishes.

Or, it is possible that some of us think of answered prayer as a kind of present we earn by "being good." While it is true that our sin may hinder the power of prayer, we do not somehow earn points so that God will hear us.

Answered prayer is not even necessarily a sign of our spiritual condition. The Apostle Paul prayed concerning a particular "thorn in the flesh":

> *Three times I pleaded with the Lord to take it away*
> *from me. But He said to me, "My grace is sufficient*
> *for you, for My power is made perfect in weakness."*
> *Therefore I will boast all the more gladly about my*

*weaknesses, so that Christ's power may rest on me
(2 Corinthians 12:8-9).*

We will not know how to pray or what to pray for, unless we understand the Scriptures. As Gary Chapman says:

> *Many people simply read the Bible, close it, and then begin praying about something totally unrelated to what they have read. Nothing could be more discourteous. We would not treat a friend like that. If a friend asks a question, we give an answer. If a friend makes a statement, we have a response; so if God speaks to us through the Bible, we should respond to what God is saying.[2]*

If our praying is not related to the Scripture and to what we can discover of the will of God through its pages, we may pray for something which is not God's best will for us.

A poignant example of this appears in the story of the Children of Israel during their journey through the desert. They grew tired of the manna God had provided—a miraculous food that contained all the nutrients the human body requires—and began to cry and plead with God to send them meat. Eventually their requests went far beyond prayer and became simple complaints. Moses finally said to them:

> *The Lord heard you when you wailed, "If only we had meat to eat! We were better off in Egypt!" Now the Lord will give you meat, and you will eat it. You will not eat it for just one day, or two days, or five, ten or twenty days, but for a whole month—until it comes out of your nostrils and you loathe it—because you have rejected the Lord, who is among you (Numbers 11:18-20).*

In recounting the event, the psalmist said, "And He gave them their request, but sent leanness into their soul" (106:15, KJV).

As a child of God, I have a right to ask Him about anything that concerns me, but I must acknowledge with humility the spiritual and emotional and physical limitations that hinder my ability to think like God thinks and understand the things God understands. And so my prayers, whether they are for the people I love, or for the people I must learn to love, must be offered in the framework of God's perfect will. I must ask God to teach me to want what He wants for me.

It may be that my prayers can make a difference in the world in a way that nothing else can.

Everybody has some sore place that needs to be healed, rough places that need to be smoothed, pockets of loneliness that need to be filled, longings that need to be expressed. I can tear open wounds, or I can apply a healing salve; I can add water to a wilting soul, or I can crush it with my carelessness. I can add flavor to the drudgery and dullness of someone's life by my prayers and my love, or I can smother praise with my complaints and make everyone else miserable. I can add light in a dark place, or I can slam all the doors and leave people blindly groping for hope and beauty and brightness. I can add salt to a world gone sour, or I can do nothing and allow Satan to take over what doesn't belong to him.

I can make a difference with my prayers.

FIFTEEN

LETTING YOURSELF OFF THE HOOK

I t wasn't enough that Marilyn's birth shattered her father's dreams of watching a son excel in football or baseball. Ironically, she would never fulfill her mother's dreams either. She was born with a disfiguring birthmark that covered her hand and arm. Hating herself and feeling the loneliness of being an outcast in her own home, Marilyn began to look elsewhere for something or someone to fill the aching void of feeling worthless.

In some perverse way, perhaps subconsciously still trying to fulfill her father's dream, Marilyn began to develop athletic skills and became a topnotch baseball player. She joined whatever leagues she could find and played in every sandlot game she could manage. Young neighborhood boys wanted her on their team, and the league teams she joined considered her their star player. Even when she finished high school and started a job, baseball was her life.

Eventully, one of her teammates introduced her to lesbianism. She didn't even know what it was called and didn't consider it to be wrong, because for the first time in her life she felt loved for herself, not for what she could do.

But her relationships changed, and the strange, aching longing she felt was never quite satisfied by the people who came and went in her life. One day, two teenage brothers who had played ball with her for years invited her to their home to meet their mother. Marilyn saw in this new friend a genuine, unselfish outpouring of love she had never experienced. The neighbors became her second family and she soon learned that their love for her came out of a deep personal relationship with a God she had thought to be unloving and unfair.

"If they really knew me," Marilyn said to herself, "they would have nothing to do with me." And so Marilyn's homosexual lifestyle remained a secret for many years.

Eventually the secret came out, and Marilyn waited for her friend to react with disgust and anger. Instead, this godly lady who had already accepted her as a daughter carefully went through the Scriptures with Marilyn and her lesbian lover, to show them God's view of homosexuality. She ended by saying, "Marilyn, I hate what you are doing, but I will never stop loving you."

How tenderly God worked in Marilyn's heart for the next few years! Even after she had accepted Christ as her Savior, the pull was strong. The homosexual churches she attended assured her that "God made her this way," that she was doing nothing wrong. But eventually, the patient teaching of her friend and the persistence of the Spirit of God started to bear fruit. Marilyn began to realize that what she had been looking for all her life was a sense of the presence of God Himself.

All the self-hatred that had marred her joy and damaged her relationships was gone. She came to the place where she could look at herself in the mirror and see a beautiful, worthwhile person redeemed by Christ's transforming power.

Now, ten years beyond that damaging lifestyle, Marilyn devotes all of her free time to helping others who seek to leave the homosexual community. She cries freely as she recounts God's great mercy to her, but her beautiful eyes sparkle through her tears as she says over and over again, "Can you believe what God has done?"

Whether or not we can identify with Marilyn's terrible sense of worthlessness, many of us struggle with a sense of inadequacy. We may measure ourselves by our failed goals or by the unrealistic expectations others have set for us. Or, perhaps we seek to hide a sense of guilt and failure—the aftermath of damage caused by our own sin or someone else's sin against us. We do not believe God could possibly love us because we do not love ourselves.

Fortunately, we do not have to muddle through life condemning ourselves and feeling condemned by God and others. When God changed the condition of our hearts, He changed our position, our status, our worth!

LETTING YOURSELF OFF THE HOOK

1. Acknowledge your own daily need for cleansing and forgiveness. It is such a simple process that we have difficulty believing it could make a difference: "If we confess our sins, He is faithful and just and will forgive us our sins and purify us from all unrighteousness. If we claim we have not sinned, we make Him out to be a liar and His word has no place in our lives (1 John 1:9-10).

Remember the story of Jesus at His last Passover, washing the feet of His disciples? Simon Peter, in a great burst of humility declared loudly, "I wouldn't consider having You wash my feet!" Of course, the problem was that he failed to understand the symbolism of what Jesus was doing.

Jesus said to him, "Unless I wash you, you have no part with Me."

With characteristic exuberance, Peter replied, "Then, Lord, not just my feet but my hands and my head as well!" (John 13:9)

Jesus' response to Peter is significant, "A person who has had a bath needs only to wash his feet; his whole body is clean." When we have been cleansed through the redeeming blood of Christ, the act of salvation does not have to be repeated. But, because we walk in a dirty world, we do need daily cleansing from those sins that advertise so loudly our frail humanity! It is only as we daily identify and confess our sins that we can experience forgiveness, that we can feel ourselves worthwhile to God and to ourselves. Sin is not an encouraging companion; it destroys our sense of value and demeans our relationship with God and man.

2. Remember your position. Is there any relationship in the world so delightful as one which includes not only understanding and acceptance, but the knowledge that there is total pleasure in the one who is loved?

And that is what God feels for His own precious child! "The Lord delights in those who fear Him, who put their hope in His unfailing love" (Psalm 147:11).

What an awesome thought, that God created you for His pleasure; He delights in your well-being! In Revelation 4:11 we read, "Thou art worthy, O Lord, to receive glory and honor and power; for Thou hast created all things, and *for Thy pleasure* they [including you!] are and were created" (KJV).

Now take it one step further. Not only are you precious to the God who created you; He has also given you rank and status—a title, no less!—to prove His love for you. In the introduction to the Book of Revelation, the Apostle John gives praise to the Lord Jesus, and then identifies our position before the throne of God, "Unto Him that loved us, and washed us from our sins in His own blood, and *hath made us kings and priests* unto God and His Father; to Him be glory and dominion for ever and ever. Amen" (1:5-6, KJV).

When you get to feeling worthless, just remember your royal position, your honorable profession!

3. Consider the price that was paid for your redemption. Measuring by human standards, how much would you say you are worth? Many years ago a Christian biologist used to say that the chemical content of the human

body was worth about 88¢! Aren't you glad your value is not measured by such a standard?

Sometimes we talk about a person's "net value" in terms of wages or income; but it would be a rather depressing thought if we became without value, simply because we lost a job or were otherwise unable to work!

Here is the real measure of your worth, "For you know that it was not with perishable things such as silver or gold that you were redeemed from the empty way of life handed down to you from your forefathers, but with the precious blood of Christ, a lamb without blemish or defect" (1 Peter 1:18-19).

How precious God considered you to be when He provided a way for you to become His child, through the death of His own beloved Son. Whatever you may consider other people's opinions to be of you, God thought you were worth the most valuable price He could pay!

It is logical to assume that if you are of great value to God, He would also consider you worth whatever investment was required to meet your needs. And that is the promise of Romans 8:32, "He who did not spare His own Son, but gave Him up for us all—how will He not also, along with Him, graciously give us all things?"

What are the channels through which God gives us His resources?

Prayer. "Do not be anxious about anything," Paul writes in Philippians 4:6-7, "but in everything, by prayer and petition, with thanksgiving, present your requests to God. And the peace of God, which transcends all understanding, will guard your hearts and your minds in Christ Jesus."

The Word of God. Joshua 1:8 says, "Do not let this Book of the Law depart from your mouth; meditate on it day and night, so that you may be careful to do everything written in it. Then you will be prosperous and successful."

Fellowship with other believers. "Let the word of Christ dwell in you richly *as you teach and admonish one an-*

other with all wisdom, and as you sing psalms, hymns and spiritual songs with gratitude in your hearts to God" (Colossians 3:16).

The power of the Holy Spirit. When the Lord Jesus was giving His disciples their final instructions before He went to the cross, He reminded them, "All this I have spoken while still with you. But the Counselor, the Holy Spirit, whom the Father will send in My name, will teach you all things and will remind you of everything I have said to you. Peace I leave with you; My peace I give you. I do not give to you as the world gives. Do not let your hearts be troubled and do not be afraid" (John 14:25-27). Daily, as we walk with God, we have a wonderful Prompter to remind us of what we are to do and how we are to live!

The healing power of praise. Can you imagine the exhaustion and fear David felt after months and months in the desert, hiding from King Saul who he knew was determined to kill him? This is a part of the psalm David wrote and sang to encourage his own heart (Psalm 57):

> *Have mercy on me, O God, have mercy on me,*
> *for in You my soul takes refuge.*
> *I will take refuge in the shadow of Your wings*
> *until the disaster has past. . . .*
> *I am in the midst of lions;*
> *I lie among ravenous beasts—*
> *men whose teeth are spears and arrows,*
> *whose tongues are sharp swords.*
> *Be exalted, O God, above the heavens;*
> *let Your glory be over all the earth. . . .*
> *My heart is steadfast, O God,*
> *my heart is steadfast;*
> *I will sing and make music.*
> *Awake, my soul! (Psalm 57:1-8)*

As obvious as David's fear is in these lines, the striking thing is that he does not end his prayer at the level of his circumstances. He praises God and exalts Him and then ends his prayer/praise by reminding his own heart to remain steady. In spite of the serious predicament in which he finds himself, he takes time to sing of the glory of God!

What would happen, I wonder, if in the dark hours of our lives we would move beyond the things that hurt and disturb us, and begin to praise and exalt the God who holds the universe in His hands?

Even if our praise were mixed with the salt of our tears, I believe we could find the comfort no other source could provide, and God would receive the honor He so richly deserves!

4. Be willing to examine your choices. Ask yourself:

"Am I making daily decisions that are producing guilt?"

"Do I regularly sacrifice my commitments for the sake of comfort or convenience?"

"Do I resist instruction and exhortation of those God has provided for my discipline and growth?"

If we never examine the areas of weakness, the "thin places" in our spiritual armor, we will keep on making the same bad choices!

5. Get off the "point system." You are not earning God's approval by the performance of a given list of duties. Stop measuring your own spiritual value by any outward activities. The Pharisees were good at mimicking the qualities of great men of God, but their behavior masked hearts that were far from God. Begin on the inside in your relationship with the Lord, and He will give you wisdom to make the outside as it ought to be.

6. Give up your need for approval from others. Nothing destroys our sense of personal value like the practice of constantly requiring others to be pleased with who we are and what we do! The Apostle Paul dared to say, "I care very little if I am judged by you or by any human court; indeed, I do not even judge myself. My conscience is clear, but that does not make me innocent. It is the Lord who judges me" (1 Corinthians 4:3-4).

"People who work as hard as I tried to do," one woman said, "always have expectations that their work will be appreciated and valued by the people around them. Of course, these unrealistic expectations are rarely met. It is difficult for anyone to satisfy people who are desperately trying to prove themselves. Relationships with people like me who have great need to be loved can be a drag!

"I have noticed, also, that it is easy for others to take advantage of 'doers'—to allow them to carry too much of the load. After all, if they want to work so hard, let them do it."

7. "Rearrange the furniture." Remove from your life-style and thought patterns the things that block your progress toward being what you want to be.

Charles was a young man struggling with long-set patterns of indulging in pornography.

"I don't like to be the way I am," he told the counselor who worked with him, "but I don't know how to resist when the 'need' comes."

When the counselor had talked with Charles long enough to chart the particular instances of temptation, he found three "pieces of furniture" in the young man's life-style that were getting in the way of spiritual healing: a private telephone in Charles' bedroom that made it easy to listen to a pornographic phone service, a night job which gave him long hours alone with nothing to do, and a broken relationship with church friends who would have provided accountability.

"Give up your private phone," the counselor advised. "Use the family phone in the kitchen when you need or want to make calls. Start looking for a daytime job that will require attention and challenge your gifts. Find a good church and begin building relationships with a responsible, mature Christian friend with whom you can share your problem. Above all, get into the Word of God so that it can give the daily protection and cleansing you need."

DEVELOPING THE FINE ART OF WAITING

Our generation is obsessed with the idea of immediate gratification. We cannot imagine life without:

Buy now—pay later credit

Drive-through car washes

Microwave ovens and frozen dinners

The "15-minute lunch" guarantee

One-day cleaning or film developing

Computer dialing.

And how about the ultimate in speed: a flight on the Concorde from Florida to London in two hours!

But God has a different view of time. "A thousand years in Your sight," the psalmist says to God, "are like a day that has just gone by."

Whatever time experts think they can do to speed up the action, there are still some things, some of the best things, that God produces in the framework of His own timing:

The nine-month gestation period for a human baby.

The development of coal and precious stones.

The producing of a great man of faith. Moses had to spend the "prime" forty years of his life waiting for a career; Abraham became a father of the promised heir at one hundred!

Are you frustrated with yourself and impatient with God because He has not yet "fixed" the things in your life and character that are keeping you from being what you want to be?

Join the club! The Apostle Paul expressed so well what I have often felt about myself:

> *I know that nothing good lives in me, that is, in my sinful nature. For I have the desire to do what is good, but I cannot carry it out. For what I do is not the good I want to do; no, the evil I do not want to do—this I keep on doing. . . . Who will rescue me from this body of death? (Romans 7:18-19, 24)*

Then Paul almost shouts the answer to his own question, *"Thanks be to God—through Jesus Christ our Lord!"* (v. 25)

The truth we have to face is that we will never measure up to what we want to be this side of eternity; but we have One who is working with us on the perfection process day by day. Here's the way Jeremiah said it, in Lamentations 3:22-26:

> *Because of the Lord's great love*
> *we are not consumed,*
>   *for His compassions never fail.*
> *They are new every morning;*
>   *great is Your faithfulness.*
> *I say to myself, "The Lord is my portion;*
>   *therefore I will wait for Him."*
> *The Lord is good to those whose hope is in Him,*
>   *to the one who seeks Him;*
> *It is good to wait quietly*
>   *for the salvation of the Lord.*

A number of years ago, when my well-ordered life was interrupted by great heartache and circumstances I could not control, I felt sure my world was collapsing. It was devastating for me to realize that my walk with the Lord was not protecting me from pain and disappointment. "Somehow," I thought, "I have missed a step in the process. The problem must be with me. If I will just buckle down and do what is right, God will fix everything quickly, and then I can go on as I did before."

But the world didn't get better, and the pain didn't go away.

In the long months that followed, I began to realize that God was, indeed, working on me, but not in the way I expected.

Patiently, day by day in the quiet recesses of my own heart, God was asking, "Am I enough? If you lost everything you considered precious except My love and My presence, could you learn to be satisfied?"

And so I waited for God to finish His work in my heart. Eventually, I was able to write the following lines to help others who were also struggling:

I Am Waiting, Lord

I am waiting, Lord,
  and I feel immobilized by fear—
Frozen by the things I do not understand.
I cannot step ahead toward goals
  that once seemed so obtainable.

Late storms have brought disaster to my landscape.
Familiar things seem somehow not to sit
  quite soundly on their old foundations.
Strange shifts of angles
  in the shape of forms
  once stable and secure
Confuse me,
  make me lose my compass point.

  Where to turn?
  What to do?

I have no clue as to the future.
My options have dissolved
  and trickle away
  with the run-off
  from the storm.

And so I wait . . .

Lord, help me not to simply sit
  among my broken things,
    turning them over and over

in my hands,
  grieving for the past.

Teach me in my waiting
  to find the valued remnants
  and store them in a place
quiet and safe.

Help me to take the time
  to bury dead dreams with dignity—
Not to wallow in regrets
  nor to collect small grievances.

Let nothing be wasted
  in this crisis that has seemed
  to stop the clock
  and lock the door
To all I felt most precious.

Help me to watch beyond my altered skyline
For that first faint glow of Morning Sun.
Let me wrap myself in faith
  and snuggle down with hope.

Help me to discern, even now,
  the soft gilding of these ruins
  with early dawn.
Let me see, approaching with the morning light,
The form of Him who stills the storm
  and transforms with His presence.[1]

And so, weary friend, struggling and impatient with the
time God is taking to make you what you want to be, it
may be that His work in your life will be accomplished
only in the context of eternity. Patiently wait for Him to
refine and polish you to make you like Himself. Do not try
to rush the process. Good things take time!

SIXTEEN

LETTING GOD
OFF THE HOOK

She was a sixteen-year-old dynamo—pretty, popular, smart, athletic—and I was puzzled when she said she needed to talk to me about the term paper she had just turned in. I had already looked it over and could tell it would be an "A" paper.

"What can I do for you, Sarah?" I asked.

"Did you get a chance to look at my paper?" Her eyes were fixed on the pencil sharpener at the corner of my desk, and she was nervously playing with her watch.

"Yes, I did. It looks like you did a great job. Tough subject—sexual abuse of children—but you've got lots of good sources, logical outline, good conclusions. Did you have a particular reason for choosing such a heavy topic?"

She looked up suddenly, eyes glittering with anger.

"Yes, I did, and that's why I wanted to talk to you. I wrote that paper because I thought it might help me understand why my stepfather did the things he did to me."

"Have you told your mother all this?"

"Oh, she knows, but I'm not sure she really believes it. You see, she's had a tough life. I don't think she could stand having to deal with what happened. Besides, all this was years ago and she probably thinks I should just forget it."

"Did writing the paper help?" I asked.

"I don't know. Until I wrote the paper, I didn't know this

kind of thing happened to so many people. I think now I'm struggling with where God was when this happened."

Her lips trembled, but her voice was steady, "Mrs. Sandberg, why would God let something like that happen to a little girl? Why did God treat me like 'poop'?"

Through the years since that conversation, I have never forgotten Sarah's question, asked in such a startling and poignant way. And I would like to say there have been times in my own life when I myself asked (much more delicately, of course!), "Lord, where are You? How could You have allowed these things to happen in my life?"

Although there are some who may struggle with the intellectual questions about God, the proof of His existence (faith vs. logic, etc.), the veracity of Scriptures, and problems involving seeming contradictions of science or history, it is probably true that *most* people struggle with far more intimate and subjective questions about God. The questions I hear people ask when they are hurting reflect the struggles they face with letting God off the hook:

1. "If God is really out there and if He really cares about my needs, why doesn't He reveal Himself to me? Why doesn't He give me some evidence of His power?"

2. "God didn't keep His promises. Didn't He say He would take care of those who put their trust in Him?"

3. "How can a good God let bad things happen?"

Whatever route we may use to answer these questions, it seems clear that the bottom line involves *learning to know God.* We can never explain why people behave the way they do unless we know them well. And we have no capacity to understand or explain God's working in our lives unless we determine to know His heart, His plan, and His basic character.

WHY DOESN'T GOD DO SOMETHING?

"If God is really out there and if He honestly cares about my needs, why doesn't He reveal Himself to me? Why doesn't He give me some evidence of His power?"

We have to remember that God isn't the one who is hiding! From the beginning of time He has designed everything in nature, in history, in the Bible, and in the Incarnation to reveal Himself.

We see God in nature. "The heavens declare the glory of God; the skies proclaim the work of His hands. Day after day they pour forth speech; night after night they display knowledge. There is no speech or language where their voice is not heard" (Psalm 19:1-3). But if we had nothing more than the structure of a tiny leaf or flower to study, we could not avoid acknowledging the presence of some Wisdom beyond our own. Walt Whitman said, "A mouse is miracle enough to stagger sextillions of infidels."

Unfortunately, when we are afraid, in trouble, or going through some great transition, we long for evidence of God's power in more direct and personal ways. We want signs and miracles; we want obvious divine intervention!

Maybe you can identify with the Israelites fleeing from the Egyptians. They had no guidebooks, no maps, no instructional videos to show them what to do or where to go. One of the ways God revealed Himself to them was in the provision of a divine night-light: "The Lord went ahead of them . . . by night in a pillar of fire to give them light, so that they could travel by day or night" (Exodus 13:21).

Then when the Egyptian army pursued them, "The angel of God, who had been traveling in front of Israel's army, withdrew and went behind them. The pillar of cloud also moved from in front and stood behind them, coming between the armies of Egypt and Israel. Throughout the night the cloud brought darkness to the one side and light to the other side" (Exodus 14:19-20).

When the Israelites had crossed the Red Sea on dry land, only to discover the Egyptian army still following, God stepped in again, for He had said, "I will gain glory through Pharaoh and all his army. . . . The Egyptians will know that I am the Lord" (vv. 17-18). The waters closed in over the Egyptians and the army was drowned. "And when the Israelites saw the great power the Lord displayed against the Egyptians, the people feared the Lord and put their trust in Him and in Moses His servant" (v. 31).

Well . . . at least for a little while!

Eventually they ran out of water, and their complaints about the scarcity of water turned into accusations about God's failure to meet their needs. When Moses finally struck the rock at the command of God, and the water gushed out, Moses reminded the people of their bad attitude. "He called the place Massah (testing) and Meribah (quarreling) because the Israelites quarreled and because they tested the Lord saying, 'Is the Lord among us or not?' " (Exodus 17:7)

No doubt the most awesome "appearance" of God to the Israelites came after He had personally dictated the Ten Commandments to Moses on Mount Sinai: "When the people saw the thunder and lightning and heard the trumpet and saw the mountain in smoke, they trembled with fear. They stayed at a distance and said to Moses (whose face was physically shining with the glory of God), 'Speak to us yourself and we will listen. But do not have God speak to us or we will die' " (Exodus 20:18-19).

It would seem that anyone who had been that close to an actual revelation of God would never doubt His presence or power. Yet, before the whole Law of God could be recorded by Moses, the Children of Israel had decided that the God who had shown them so many miracles, who day by day had given evidence of His presence, was not real. They said to Aaron, "Come, make us gods who will go before us. As for this fellow Moses who has brought us up out of Egypt, we don't know what has happened to him" (Exodus 32:1).

The question we have to ask ourselves is whether our doubts about the presence of God in our daily lives would be basically altered if we had ways to see Him with our eyes or touch Him with our hands.

The disciples spent nearly every waking hour of their lives for more than three years, in the presence of Deity; yet when testing came, they doubted that what they had seen and heard was God.

It is not the fiery manifestation of God in a burning bush that we need to see, or the presence of an angelic being. If God took human form and walked among us today, we still might doubt His personal concern for the things that trouble us.

And yet, that divine concern is exactly what we want and need. To *feel* the presence of God in our daily lives is the unspoken and often unrecognized hunger of every human heart. But it is not God who has built the wall or fogged the glass so that we cannot see Him.

Just as He visited Adam and Eve in the cool of the evening, so He wants intimate fellowship with us.

Just as He watched over the Children of Israel in the fiery pillar of cloud by night, so He hovers over His own in the dark desert places of our lives.

Just as He shone through the face of Moses, thundered from the mountain of His Law, smiled through the rainbow of grace for Noah, walked with Enoch, whispered to Elijah, and mingled His tears with those of Mary and Martha, God wants to reveal Himself to you and me.

But we have something more than these saints of God had—we have accesss to the written Word of God. We are not limited to the reading and interpretation of the Bible by some human authority; we can hold in our hands and read with our own eyes the very Word of God, and we have the Holy Spirit within us to give sense and meaning. In our struggles to understand where God is and what He is doing, we can daily turn to the pages of Scripture to see Him at work in the lives of those who have gone before us, and we can read again the promises of what He intends to do for us. We do not have to depend on a dream, an angelic appearance, a burst of fire, or a pillar of cloud to know that God is with us.

Even though we have the Word of God, we still struggle with a kind of spiritual myopia. Our own humanity and our sin limit our vision and obscure the image of God. But that will not always be true, thank God! Paul tells us, "Now we see but a poor reflection as in a mirror; then we shall see face to face. Now I know in part; then I shall know fully, even as I am fully known" (1 Corinthians 13:12).

WHY DOESN'T GOD KEEP HIS PROMISES?

"Does God always keep His promises? Don't I have a right to expect things to go well, if I am doing what God has told me to do?"

Our confusion comes from our limited perspective. We don't see how God, running on His track of a perfect plan and a perfect will, can accomplish what He has promised to do, while the forces of evil are constantly working at blowing up the tracks!

The ultimate design for our lives is that God will get glory for Himself, as He leads us toward our final destination of perfection and fellowship with Him. God is not distracted by our poor choices, and His will is not sabotaged by the evil other people do to us. While He is perfect and His plan is perfect, He knows how to make accommodation to the human frailties of those through whom He has chosen to accomplish His purposes.

Does the word "accommodation" bother you? Does it seem that somehow God is not quite in charge of the universe, if He has to work around human failure? Remember that God "allowed" sin in His perfect world. It did not take Him by surprise and He did not have to hurriedly come up with a plan to counterattack it when it first invaded Eden. Before time began, God determined that He wanted the *willing* love and obedience and fellowship of persons on whom He could dispense His great love and grace and pleasure.

If God had designed us as robots, to worship and serve Him without personal commitment and choice, what kind of fellowship would that have provided? Because God allowed for the possibility of sin, and of personal choice, He knows how to use these in accomplishing His will!

God's work in developing Moses as leader was not sidetracked when Moses begged God to use Aaron as his "mouthpiece." God's promises to give Abraham and Sarah a son, from whose line the Redeemer would come, were not limited by the birth of Ishmael. God works with, not in spite of, human frailty or failure.

The beautiful song, "All Things Work for Our Good" by Eddie Carswell and Babbie Mason, reminds us:

> All things work for our good,
> Though sometimes we can't see how they could.
> Struggles that break our hearts in two
> Sometimes blind us from the truth.
> Our Father knows what's best for us;
> His ways are not our own.
> So when your pathway grows dim
> And you just can't see Him,
> Remember He's still on the throne.
>
> He sees the master plan.
> He holds our future in His hands,
> So don't live as those who have no hope.
> All our hope is found in Him.
>
> We walk in present knowledge
> But He sees the first and the last,
> And like a tapestry He's weaving
> You and me to someday be just like Him. . . .
>
> God is too wise to be mistaken;
> God is too good to be unkind.
> For when you don't understand,

When you don't see His plan,
When you can't trace His hand,
Trust His heart.[1]

WHY DOES GOD LET BAD THINGS HAPPEN?

"How can a good God let bad things happen to good people, to innocent people, to helpless people?"

If we are going to "trust His heart," then we have to genuinely know the Person in whom we put that trust.

We could, of course, list all the attributes of God, as we find them in the pages of Scripture, and that would certainly be a valuable thing to do. But we need to go a step further; we need to see how the person of God is tied in with the things we see happening around us, particularly the difficult and painful things that touch our own lives.

There is something heart-wrenching about on-the-spot coverage of the world's disasters. The accessibility of the media to the distant reaches of the earth allows us to see people being dragged out of the rubble of earthquakes. We see the devastation of tornado or hurricane. We watch the destruction of homes and property and lives by fire or flood or the ravages of war. There is no privacy for the tears and shock and disbelief of the victims, as they stumble through the wreckage of places once familiar and safe.

How in the world does all this fit in with the characteristics of a God who is fair and loving, all-knowing and all-powerful? We can get a little clue in looking at the story of God's people Israel, as they were slaughtered and raped and taken captive by foreign nations. Lonely, puzzled, and afraid, they asked the same questions you and I ask, "Lord, where are You? How could You let this happen to Your own?"

But God does not forget His own, and the day came when the chains were removed and the edict was announced: the Israelites were to go home to their own country.

Can you picture Nehemiah and Ezra, trying to reconstruct the broken walls and broken lives of the little band who, with such great hope, had left the land of their captivity to return to Jerusalem? The shady streets, the olive gardens, and the bustling marketplaces were all gone. Dust and rubbish were everywhere, and each attempt to restore order and safety was ridiculed by their enemies who hoped to see them fail.

It had been so long since these Jews had heard the Word of God or knelt before His altar; their lifestyle reflected not the teaching of their fathers but the wicked practices of their pagan captors.

Nehemiah decided it was time for them to remember not only their own heritage, but also the attributes of the God who loved them and had brought them home. For one entire day, they listened to the ancient Law that was almost forgotten. So amazed were they at what they heard that they first lifted their hands and responded, " 'Amen! Amen!' Then they bowed down and worshiped the Lord with their faces to the ground" (Nehemiah 8:6).

When they had wept and rejoiced and reestablished the celebration of the seven-day Feast of Tabernacles, Ezra ended the ceremony with this significant prayer:

> Blessed be Your glorious name, and may it be exalted above all blessing and praise. You alone are the Lord. You made the heavens, even the highest heavens, and all their starry host, the earth, and all that is on it, the seas and all that is in them. You give life to everything, and the multitudes of heaven worship You.
>
> You are the Lord God, who chose Abram. . . . You found his heart faithful to You, and You made a covenant with him. . . . You have kept Your promise because You are righteous.
>
> You saw the suffering of our forefathers in Egypt; You heard their cry at the Red Sea. You sent miracu-

lous signs and wonders against Pharaoh, against all his officials and all the people of his land, for You knew how arrogantly the Egyptians treated them. You made a name for Yourself, which remains to this day. You divided the sea before them, so that they passed through it on dry ground. . . .

You came down on Mount Sinai; You spoke to them from heaven. . . .

But they, our forefathers, became arrogant and stiff-necked, and did not obey Your commands. They refused to listen, and failed to remember the miracles You performed among them. . . . But You are a forgiving God, gracious and compassionate, slow to anger and abounding in love. Therefore You did not desert them, even when they cast for themselves an image of a calf and said, "This is your god." So You handed them over to their enemies, who oppressed them. But when they were oppressed they cried out to You. From heaven You heard them, and in Your great compassion You gave them deliverers, who rescued them. . . .

In Your great mercy you did not put an end to them or abandon them, for You are a gracious God (Nehemiah 9:5-11, 13, 16-18, 27, 31).

When we read this cause-and-effect account of Israel's early history, the patterns and the plan seem clear. We can see how God used His hand of judgment to bring His people back to Himself.

Our own personal history is a lot harder to read. We can see what has happened, but neither the process of God's plan for us nor the ultimate goal is totally discernible. If we do not have confidence in the One who controls the plan, then the events of our lives may appear senseless.

Forty years ago, when my husband and I were married, we had engraved inside our wedding rings, "Psalm 37." In the glow of our dreams for serving the Lord, we especially related to verse 4, "Delight yourself in the Lord and He will give you the desires of your heart."

What a wonderful verse on which to build a life! But there are dark shadows that flit across the biographical pages of us all, even of the "righteous." Verse 12 says, "The wicked plot against the righteous and gnash their teeth at them; but the Lord laughs at the wicked, for He knows their day is coming."

Here's where the hard part comes! We can always look backward in history to see whether or not things have "turned out right;" but when we are living today at the bottom of the pit, it is hard to see how God is in the process of meeting the desires of our hearts! We haven't come to the last chapter; we can't see the "happily ever after" ending to what God is doing.

Verses 23 and 24 explain it a little further, "If the Lord delights in a man's way, He makes his steps firm; though he stumble, he will not fall, for the Lord upholds him with His hand."

When God designed my life for blessing and usefulness, He did not preclude the possibility of my stumbling. Nor is He unaware of the very real fact that my stumbling, as well as the stumbling of those on whom I lean, will result in pain and suffering. The scars of our human condition can't be hidden. We have been crippled by living in a corrupted world.

But God never gives up on us, and He never throws us away; He "upholds us with His hand." Better yet, the very scars which shame us and grieve us, He often uses for our good. Whether or not our lives have been damaged by our own sin, by the circumstances we could not control, or by the deliberate evil of one who intended to hurt us, God does not waste any of it. God, the great Recycler of the universe, takes all the garbage and loss and limitation and pain and turns them into something that will be for His glory and our greatest good.

In *Walking on Water*, Madeleine L'Engle says:

It is interesting to note how many artists have had physical problems to overcome, deformities, lameness, terrible loneliness. Could Beethoven have written that glorious paean of praise in the Ninth Symphony if he had not had to endure the dark closing in of deafness? . . . Could Milton have seen all that he sees in Paradise Lost *if he had not been blind? It is chastening to realize that those who have no physical flaw, who move through life in step with their peers, who are bright and beautiful, seldom become artists. The unending paradox is that we do learn through pain.*[2]

We probably never will see clearly what God has in mind while we are going through the processes of His most significant work in our lives, but someday it will be made perfectly plain to us what He was doing all along! Someday, when I awake in the presence of the One who planned for me both the tears and the triumphs, I will be glad for all the tools He used to shape me for His glory!

"And I—in righteousness I will see Your face; when I awake, I will be satisfied with seeing Your likeness" (Psalm 17:15).

SEVENTEEN

LOVE: THE ULTIMATE REVENGE

M ost of us have had times in our lives when we were hurt so badly that it was difficult not to think of some kind of revenge. Even if we did not actually plot what we would do—if we could get away with it—in those dark moments of anger we pictured how good it would feel if God would just "zap" the person who had hurt us!

Perhaps we simply planned our own unforgiveness to be a kind of revenge! We fully hoped that the person who had done us wrong would never be able to look us in the eye without having to remember that he "did us dirt"!

Maybe you can identify with one woman's struggle for revenge.

KAREN'S STORY

Even though it was my favorite place to eat, tonight the music seemed much too loud and the food utterly taste-less. Dick was the one who had suggested we come here to work out the problem between us.

It wasn't exactly a neutral place. We had celebrated too many high points in this very room and shared too much laughter for it to be considered anywhere near neutral. But at least it was not a place that held the echoes of our recent angry words or the memory of sharp looks and bitter tears.

"How can you consider throwing away thirty years of a good marriage?" Dick asked. There was pleading in his eyes.

"How could *you* have jeopardized a thirty-year marriage?" I countered.

"Karen, we've been through all that. I've told you how sorry I am. I love you. You are the *only* one I love. You are the only one I have *ever* loved."

Forgiveness had been uncomplicated the first time. If a man has been faithful for twenty-five years of marriage, you can chalk up one sudden, embarrassingly indiscreet relationship to a midlife crisis. The fact that Dick had not ever been known to be secretive only proved that there had not been a long-contemplated deception. It had just happened. I had read enough and comforted other friends often enough to know that even a good man might become vulnerable at a time when he is struggling with doubts about his own lost youth and unfinished dreams.

But the second episode did not seem so forgivable. It couldn't really be called an affair, because the young woman was a friend of mine, and it was she who blurted out the humiliating details of Dick's attempted seduction.

My rage had frightened me. I heard the sound of my own voice, as though some stunned silent part of me down inside were listening with horror to the anger and hurt that came pouring out.

People always said Dick and I had a lot to show for our long marriage. We had shared many things—gardening, travel, music, and, of course, our wonderful children. Connie and Joe with their two gifted little ones were an easy five hours away. Dickie and his Alice shared a wide farmhouse with their precious babies, halfway across the country.

"People always said . . ." Ah, *that* was the problem!

All my life I had been working hard to build the perfect

marriage, the ideal family, the most gracious home. All my life, I had fit the bits and pieces of my dreams in place to hide the shame and humiliation of never quite being able to measure up to the standards of my perfectionist father.

I had tried to make small happinesses out of the fabric of daily schedule—my garden, good books, a few hours each week on the violin, a joyful hospitality; now my hopes and dreams sat in the glass jars of my mind, unjelled and tasteless.

'Dick's voice finally brought me back to the restaurant, the uneaten meal, the silence between us.

"Karen, talk to your mother before you do anything."

"How could you suggest such a thing? You know as well as I do that my mother is a perfect saint. She would be horrified to know what has been going on with us. She thinks we're the perfect couple.

"In fact," I couldn't help adding, vindictively, "you know she thinks you are the best thing that ever happened to me. What would she say if she knew . . . if she knew . . ." My voice broke.

In frustration I blew my nose on the linen napkin and stood up. "Let's go home," I said. "This music is giving me a headache."

My garden got a lot of special attention that week. There is something cleansing and healing about digging into the soil and pulling weeds and watching seedlings show their tiny heads.

My mind kept going back to that last session with the psychologist. I was the one who had insisted that Dick get counseling, but I was finding the process more difficult than I had expected. Just last week, the counselor had asked to talk to both of us together. Even the memory of that humiliating hour made me yank out a weed so hard it almost threw me over backward.

"Dick tells me that you are having a hard time forgiving him," Dr. Stevens had said.

"That's not really true," I said. "Even though I was very,

very angry, I did tell him that I forgave him. It's just that I don't trust him. The more we talk about this, the more details I am discovering about patterns that leave me feeling very uneasy. How can I ever be sure that he won't do this again?"

Dr. Stevens had paused only a moment before he said, "You can't. You could divorce Dick, and that may be what you want to do; but if you are going to stay in the marriage, you can't be an avenging parent who says by her attitude, 'You are a naughty boy and I will keep punishing you so that you will never do this again!' Until you can rebuild your trust in Dick, you will have to learn to trust God, who loves *you* whether *you* are trustworthy or not."

I left Dr. Stevens' office with a murmured, "Thank you," and a courteous handshake, but I felt a hopelessness down inside. "It really isn't fair," I thought. "Why is it the injured party, the innocent one, has to feel guilty? Why is it I have to take all the responsibility for the reconciliation?"

It was a wet, dismal summer. Although my garden flourished, nothing I did during those dark days seemed profitable or beautiful. Every morning Dick brought me a cup of coffee and said, "I love you." I accepted the coffee with a word of thanks and I returned the kiss, but I could not force myself to step across the chasm of my own pain to restore the relationship Dick and I had once enjoyed.

Daily, I watched him spend more and more time alone with the Word of God, and I recognized Dick's increasing attempts to anticipate my needs and lighten my burden. Although I did all the "right" things and tried desperately to say all the "right" things, the little knot of bitterness stayed hot and tight inside my heart. By the end of the summer I was exhausted with depression and despair.

Finally I got the courage to attempt some kind of positive action. "Dick, if you don't mind," I said, "I think maybe I should go see my mother for a couple of days. She's been asking me to come."

Was there a flicker of hope in Dick's eyes? "By all means, go and spend time with her. I can take care of things here. Jack has asked me to help him put on a new roof," he said. "I'll keep busy."

Later that evening as Mom and I sat at her kitchen table drinking tea, she reached out and took my hand.

"Now tell me," she said without any preliminaries, "about you and Dick."

"How did you know. . . ?"

"Dick told me—weeks ago."

I dropped my head and let the accumulated summer of pain spill out in my tears and voice and clenched fists until there was nothing left to say.

My mother wiped her own tears, patted my hand, and then said, "I've been praying, and I've decided it is time for me to tell you a story I've never told anyone."

She paused to chuckle. "You know what your dad was like—a wonderful man but, well . . . pretty demanding. He always knew what he wanted done and how he wanted it done. Remember, though, that he grew up without a mother to brag on him and I think that because of that, he never knew how to make other people feel valuable."

"When we had been married a few years—you were just a little girl—I began to get angrier and angrier because I felt I could never please him. I thought it was obvious he didn't love me, and although I would never have considered divorce, I did sort of want to make your father 'wake up' and notice that I was a valuable person. I won't go into the details, but there was a man at the church we attended who was definitely 'coming on' to me—is that the way you say it? Anyway, I kept thinking how nice it would be to have a man in my life who thought I was wonderful and didn't mind showing it."

My mother paused and studied her hands for a minute "This is pretty difficult to talk about. What I did was . . . well . . . I actually met this man out at a forest preserve and I let him kiss me."

At that point I wanted to put my hand over my mother's mouth and say, "No! No! Don't tell me any more! Why are you telling me this?" In fact, I was so stunned I couldn't say anything. This was my saintly mother talking!

"When that man kissed me," my mother finally continued, "I suddenly realized what I was doing. I ran to my car sobbing, cried all the way home, and I never spoke to the man again.

"You see," she said simply, "Dick and I are in the same boat. We tried to fill the deepest longings of our hearts in the wrong way."

I was speechless, but I was nervous too. It was easy to see now where this was going.

"And now, my dear," my mother continued, "what are we going to do about you? Dick needs you and you are going to have to decide whether you are going to meet his need or whether you are simply going to give up, because you can't have that perfect unflawed marriage you thought you had a right to expect.

"In some ways, my sin was worse than Dick's," Mom said, "because I actually planned an affair. I *wanted* to hurt your dad, and although adultery never took place, I had already been adulterous in my heart, and in God's eyes it is the same thing. Dick never planned to do wrong. He was not prepared to face the temptation and when it came, he fell.

"Karen, the issue here is whether you are willing to let God be God. You remember in the Sermon on the Mount Jesus gave us what we call 'The Lord's Prayer.' At the end of the prayer, Jesus added, 'If you forgive men when they sin against you, your Heavenly Father will also forgive you. But if you do not forgive men their sins, your Father will not forgive your sins.' "

I had heard enough. Suddenly all the bitterness and despair began to melt. I saw the shabbiness of my own hurt pride and finally realized how tightly I had held on to my need to be "right." I had made a practice of daily rip-

ping off the emotional bandages to examine my wounded
heart and was refusing to allow it to heal.

At last we picked up our cups of cold tea and dumped
them in the sink. I felt as though I had been away from
home for weeks.

There was one more question to ask. "Mom, did Dad
ever know? And was he different after that? I always
thought he was rather proud of you."

"No, I don't think he ever knew, but he did begin to
change. Of course, he was always something of a perfectionist, you know, but when I started learning how to depend on the Lord for my sense of value, your dad seemed
to see me in a different light. We really did end up having a
pretty good marriage."

"Yes, I know . . . I know. . . . Mom, would you mind very
much if I went home tomorrow? Maybe Dick and I could
come back to see you together . . . real soon. I think I'd
like to call Dick."

I suddenly realized my heart was beating fast with an-
ticipation, waiting for the sound of his voice at the other
end of the line. "Dick," I said. "it's me. I decided to come
home tomorrow . . . and Dick . . . I love you."

LOVE IS THE ANSWER

In the end, there is one quality and one alone that will
make forgiveness possible, and that is love.

Logic certainly won't work. Logic says, "Stupid person!
Doesn't he know he's going to have to deal with the way he
has treated me eventually?"

Justice says, "He's got to pay for what he did."

Character says, "It isn't fair, but I'll have to learn to put
up with it."

Even Mercy, tenderest of all virtues, says with a sigh,
"He's a bad person and he has hurt me, but I will forgive
him."

Only Love, and her twin sister, Grace, can say, "You are

valuable to me just as you are, without regard to the past or the future. My acceptance of you is beyond guilt. It is even beyond change of heart or reformation of character."

Love simply forgives. Whatever consequences the sinner has to pay for his sin (and sin *does* have its consequences!), they are not a part of the forgiveness contract.

Take, for example, the story of the rich young ruler in the Gospel of Mark. Here was a young man who turned his back on Jesus because he could not bear to pay the cost of discipleship. In the middle of this story is the poignant comment, "Jesus looked at him and loved him" (10:21). Didn't Jesus *know* that the young man was going to reject Him? Would He have loved him anyway? Did Jesus *stop* loving the young man after he turned and walked away?

The answers to these questions are important because they give us clues to the character of God. We can never get away from the fact that God's love has no relationship to worthiness. And if we are going to forgive like God forgives, we must know what kind of God we have.

The character of God requires forgiving the unforgivable. The character of God includes the capacity to love the unlovable, to give love that may not be returned or rewarded.

When Jesus died on the cross, one of His last communications with the Father was this, "Father, forgive them; for they know not what they are doing" (Luke 23:34). Our response to those who have hurt us is apt to be, "Yeah, but this guy knew *exactly* what he was doing. He intended to do me wrong!" What we have a hard time realizing is that sin is blind. It plunges ahead creating havoc, both unable and unwilling to face the consequences.

The problem is, that if the evil or thoughtless deeds people commit against us reflect "blindness," then unforgiveness does too!

Anyone who claims to be in the light but hates his
brother is still in the darkness. Whoever loves his

brother lives in the light, and there is nothing in him
to make him stumble. But whoever hates his brother
is in the darkness and walks around in the darkness;
he does not know where he is going, because the
darkness has blinded him (1 John 2:9-11).

Evil always comes out of the blindness of hatred. No wonder Jesus said, "Father forgive them, for they know not what they do." There is a sense in which the person who does wrong really does stumble around in the darkness of his sin, doing damage he is not even capable of imagining. And while we are dealing with the painful result of someone else's sin, we must ask ourselves if we are willing to get out of the darkness of our own hate and walk in the light of God's love.

In the end, all of us have to face the fact that if we are going to be able to forgive, we will have to learn to love as God loves. "If anyone says, 'I love God,' yet hates his brother, he is a liar. For anyone who does not love his brother, whom he has seen, cannot love God, whom he has not seen. And He has given us this command: Whoever loves God must also love his brother" (1 John 4:20-21).

The great miraculous eraser that makes forgiveness possible is formed by our hunger to know God and to walk in His presence and with His power. We cannot manufacture forgiveness out of great determination or through the simple process of forgetting.

There is a point we must come to in which we choose, deliberately and perhaps repeatedly, to let go of our right to be angry, of our right to exact payment for the hurt someone else has inflicted on us. We must choose to be like the Lord Jesus Himself, to love as He loved, to forgive as He forgave.

And that is the ultimate revenge. For when we choose to love as Jesus Himself loved, we take away the power of the one who hurt us. Whether the offense was intentional or merely careless, forgiveness removes us from the place of

helpless victimization to the place of choice and freedom.
The very weapon Satan intended to cause us discouragement and pain (or worse!) we can turn into an opportunity
to be like Jesus Christ Himself.

> God wants us to be courageous people who are deep-
> ly bothered by the horrors of living as a part of a
> fallen race, people who look honestly at every strug-
> gle, who feel overwhelmed by what we see, yet
> emerge prepared to live. Scarred, still troubled, but
> deeply loving. When the fact is faced that life is pro-
> foundly disappointing, the only way to make it is to
> learn to love. And only those who are no longer con-
> sumed with finding satisfaction now are able to love.
> Only when we commit our yearnings for perfect joy
> to a Father we have learned to deeply trust are we
> free to live for others, despite the reality of a perpetu-
> al ache.[1]

NOTES

Chapter One
1. Arthur W. Pink, *Gleanings in Genesis* (Chicago: Moody Press, 1922), 54–55. Used by permission.

Chapter Two
1. David A. Seamands, *Freedom from the Performance Trap* (Wheaton, Illinois: Victor Books, 1988), 147.
2. J.S. Schmidt, "Jewish Couple Leads Rites for Klansman Who Rejected Hate," *The Chattanooga Times* (10 September 1992), A7.
3. Thomas á Kempis, *The Imitation of Christ: Selections* (Brewster, New York: Fleming H. Revell Company, 1953), 52.

Chapter Three
1. Frederick Buechner, Exact source unknown.
2. Bob Phillips, *The Delicate Art of Dancing with Porcupines* (Ventura, California: Regal Books, 1989), 135–36.

Chapter Four
1. Karen Dockrey, *From Frustration to Freedom: Ten*

Studies on the Book of Romans (Wheaton, Illinois: Victor Books, 1992), 24.

2. David A. Seamands, *Freedom from the Performance Trap* (Wheaton, Illinois: Victor Books, 1988), 130.

3. Dan B. Allender, *The Wounded Heart: Hope for Adult Victims of Sexual Abuse* (Colorado Springs: NavPress, 1990), 179.

4. Kristin A. Kunzman, *The Healing Way: Adult Recovery from Childhood Sexual Abuse* (Center City, Minnesota: Hazelden Publishers, 1990), 125–26.

5. Stephen R. Covey, *The Seven Habits of Highly Effective People: Powerful Lessons in Personal Change* (New York: Simon & Schuster, Inc., 1989), 196.

Chapter Five
1. H. Norman Wright, *Crisis Counseling* (Nashville: Here's Life Publishers, Inc., 1985), 147.

2. James Johnson, *Loneliness Is Not Forever* (Chicago: Moody, 1979), 72.

3. Walter Henrichsen, *How to Disciple Your Children* (Wheaton, Illinois: Victor Books, 1983), 54.

4. David A. Seamands, *Healing for Damaged Emotions* (Wheaton, Illinois: Victor Books, 1981), 85.

Chapter Six
1. Philip Elmer-DeWitt, "Cloning: Where Do We Draw the Line?" *Time* (8 November 1993), 65.

2. Ibid., 65.

3. Bill Cosby, *Love and Marriage* (New York: Bantam Books, 1989), 207–8.

4. Tim LaHaye, *Why You Act the Way You Do* (Wheaton, Illinois: Tyndale House Publishers, Inc., 1984), 238.

5. Ibid., 231.

6. Kevin Leman, *The Birth Order Book* (Brewster, New York: Fleming H. Revell Company, 1991), 64.

7. Ibid., 184.
8. Christine Gorman, "Sizing Up the Sexes" *Time* (20 January 1992), 42.

Chapter Seven

1. Erwin W. Lutzer, *When a Good Man Falls* (Wheaton, Illinois: Victor Books, 1985), 129.

Chapter Eight

1. Edith Schaeffer, *Affliction* (Brewster, New York: Fleming H. Revell Company, 1978), 109, 115.
2. Isobel Kuhn, *In the Arena* (Littleton, Colorado: OMF Books, 1960), 90.
3. Corrie ten Boom, *Prison Letters* (Carmel, New York: Guideposts, 1975), 81.

Chapter Nine

1. Grace MacMullen, *Pain: The Gift Nobody Wants* (Chattanooga, Tennessee: Joyful Christian Ministries, 1980), 16.
2. John R. Rice, Letter to author, 20 March 1951.

Chapter Ten

1. Ruth Harms Calkin, *Lord, It Keeps Happening . . . and Happening* (Wheaton, Illinois: Tyndale House Publishers, Inc., 1984), 90. Used by permission.

Chapter Eleven

1. David Augsburger, *The Freedom of Forgiveness* (Chicago: Moody Press, 1970), 68.
2. Lloyd Ogilvie, *Twelve Steps to Living without Fear* (Waco, Texas: Word, 1987), 57.

3. David Seamands, *Freedom from the Performance Trap* (Wheaton, Illinois: Victor Books, 1988), 180.

4. Gary Rosberg, *Choosing to Love Again* (Colorado Springs: Focus on the Family Publications, 1992), 226.

5. David Augsburger, *The Freedom of Forgiveness* (Chicago: Moody, 1970), 68.

6. Everett L. Worthington, Jr., *Marriage Counseling* (Downers Grove, Illinois: InterVarsity Press, 1989), 293.

Chapter Twelve

1. Robert Hemfelt, Frank Minirth, Paul Meier, *Love Is a Choice* (Nashville: Thomas Nelson, Inc., 1989), 232–33.

2. Paul W. Powell, *When the Hurt Won't Go Away* (Wheaton, Illinois: Victor Books, 1989), 124.

3. Gary Rosberg, *Choosing to Love Again: Restoring Broken Relationships* (Colorado Springs: Focus on the Family Publishing, 1992), 215. All rights reserved. Copyright secured. Used by permission.

4. Robert S. McGee and Pat Springle, *Getting Unstuck: Help for People Bogged Down in Recovery* (Houston and Dallas: Rapha Publishing/Word, Inc., 1992), 187.

5. H. Norman Wright, *Crisis Counseling* (Nashville: Here's Life Publishers, Inc., 1985), 77–78.

Chapter Thirteen

1. Stephen Brown, *When Your Rope Breaks* (Nashville: Thomas Nelson, Inc., 1988), 15.

2. Norman M. Lobensz, "What Do You Want from Your Marriage?" *Woman's Day* (July 1973), 36.

3. Walter A. Henrichsen, *How to Disciple Your Children* (Wheaton, Illinois: Victor Books, 1981), 62.

4. Kevin Huggins, *Parenting Adolescents* (Colorado Springs: NavPress, 1989), 20.

5. Ibid., 74.

Chapter Fourteen
1. John R. Rice, *God's Cure for Anxious Care* (Murfreesboro, Tennessee: Sword of the Lord Publishers, 1944), 16–17.
2. Gary Chapman, *Hope for the Separated* (Chicago: Moody, 1982), 46.

Chapter Fifteen
1. Jessie R. Sandberg, "I Am Waiting, Lord," *The Joyful Woman* (July/August 1990), 12.

Chapter Sixteen
1. Eddie Carswell and Babbie Mason, "Trust His Heart" (Nashville: Word Music, 1988).
2. Madeleine L'Engle, *Walking on Water* (Wheaton, Illinois: Harold Shaw Publishers, 1980), 62–63.

Chapter Seventeen
1. Larry Crabb, *Inside Out* (Colorado Springs: NavPress, 1988), 19.